Dream
Yourself Awake

Dream
Yourself Awake

One woman's Journey to uncover
her divine purpose through dreams

Darlene Montgomery

Lifedreams Publishing
Toronto, Canada

Canadian Cataloguing in Publication Data
Montgomery, Darlene 1958–
Dream Yourself Awake:
a dream is a doorway leading back to yourself.

ISBN 0-9683402-0-2
1. Self-actualization (Psychology) 2. Dream Interpretation
1. Title
Bf1091.M65 1999   158.1   C99-901444-7

Cover Art and Layout by Julie Olson
Painting oil on canvas 16" by 20":
Russel's Inner Passage by Julie Olson

Editing by: Marina Quattrocchi and Bill Belfontaine

Textual design and layout: Karen Petherick

Printed in Canada

Acknowledgements

In the process of writing *Dream Yourself Awake*, I have had an immense amount of guidance and assistance from friends and experts without whom this book could not have been completed.

Thanks to Shelley Drayton who coached me through the first stages of editing by giving loving advice and support.

Thanks to Marina Quattrocchi who had a profound impact on the completion of this book. She believed in the importance of dreams and had just the right approach with her editing. Jane Durst Pulkys, Jeff and Gwen King, Sharon Lee Chappelle, Rick McCormick and Raymond Aaron all assisted me by reading the manuscript and offering heartfelt encouragement.

Thanks to Linda Anderson of *Angel Animals* and Raymond Aaron, Co-author of *Chicken Soup for the Canadian* and *Parent's Soul* for their testimonials. Thanks to the Inner Master, Wah Z, for ongoing support through dreams and inner guidance.

A special thanks to Julie Olson for her time and cover artwork, including the painting titled, "Russel's Inner Passage". Her dedication to her art, and her commitment to living her own dreams is truly inspirational.

A special thanks to Karen Petherick for her special touches on formatting and special final touches on the cover. Thanks to Bill Belfontaine who went beyond the call of duty with his editing. Thanks also to Janet Matthews whose editing helped to polish the final product.

Thanks to all who encouraged me by purchasing a copy of this book before it was completed and to all who kept me going through asking and continuing to ask when it would be finished.

Darlene Montgomery   V

Contents

Dream
Yourself Awake

There is a vitality, a life force, an energy,
a quickening, that is translated through you into
action, and because there is only one of you in all
time, this expression is unique.

Martha Graham

My Field of Dreams

Years ago, I had a dream in which I met with Oprah Winfrey. At first I was unclear about just exactly what her presence in my dreams might mean. The Oprah Winfrey Show was still in its early years, and had not yet evolved into the profound instrument of spirit it was later to become. It was long before the general public, including myself had become familiar with her, and her mission.

As time passed, she returned many times, and I became accustomed to her regular visits. At some point I began to realize this image of Oprah was there to teach me about myself. She became a dream mentor, helping me to form an internal vortex from which a brand new self within me could take shape.

As seasons came and went, I grew to realize that Oprah's appearance in my dreams was intended to awaken me to my own potential as a voice of change in this world. But how was I to do this?

The challenge, I learned was in becoming more and more myself and less influenced by the "social consciousness" of our

Darlene Montgomery

time. By that I mean the barrage of concepts, strategies and ideas that our modern culture presents as the best way to live, think and be. What followed was a war, in fact a raging battle within myself as the outer world seemed to taunt me to get in pace with the pressure of performing for the crowds.

Deep in my heart, I heard the inner voice saying: "Just tell your stories." It seemed too simple an approach. Spirit would keep me to this path of simplicity and telling stories, but first I fought an inner battle that was only apparent to myself.

My dreams began to play an even larger part in shedding light on what my true path in life was to be. The more I worked with them, the more they began to reveal. My dreams gradually opened my eyes to a vision of life ever unfolding and flowering into something more beautiful and mysterious than I had ever imagined possible.

As I learned to decipher the symbols and patterns of my own dream language, I saw that they drew a pathway through my life, much like a beacon guiding me ever onward to a purpose. At first, this purpose was totally unknown, but as time passed, it became clearer and clearer.

The story begins with an introduction to the causes of my deep inner struggle and search for wholeness and freedom. It was through my dreams that I first learned of the "Eastern Parasite," an entity locked within myself which fed off destructive habits and outdated beliefs from lifetimes gone by.

This parasite stole energy by siphoning off my will to live and accept good in my life. It came in a number of disguises, which confused my efforts to fully identify it and release its hold on me.

I came to realize that my mission was obscured and blocked from manifesting by the underlying deep-rooted patterns induced by this entity, and that overcoming them wouldn't be easy.

When I first asked to know my mission, it set off an unconscious mechanism inside me. The direction of my life changed simply from asking the question. Past choices made from that place of obscured vision had influenced my emotional states and many of the resulting issues needed to be faced again and again so that I could gain greater spiritual and emotional strength.

My dreams also showed my future, many times letting me know the importance of decisions I was making in my life. I was often *compelled* to listen to inner directions, though it wasn't always clear why I needed to follow them. Learning to trust my inner directions was a deep lesson of my heart and many times a painful one.

Over the years my dreams of Oprah would return again and again, until I understood that – *Oprah was me*, the real me or Soul – encased within the parasite shell. Soul is the real self. We don't just have a soul. We *are* Soul, an eternal being, who is seeking to recall Its' mission as a co-worker with God.

Accepting this profound truth would take far longer than I imagined, but the journey carved the way for others to benefit from my experiences.

To write a book is to open a door literally into another world. Every work of art leaves an impression, which shapes the thoughts of others and more importantly their dreams. To fulfill our destiny, we must pass through the veil of social acceptance, not usually easy, and finally embrace our vision.

One day we look up and realize our vision has become the present reality.

It took many years and untold painful moments to peel away the layers of fear preventing me from knowing the truth and accepting my mission.

Darlene Montgomery

"When a man takes a step toward God, God takes more steps toward that man than there are sands in the world of time."

The Work of the Chariot

A Circle of Geese

How does one begin the journey of finding their mission in life?

Many of us pass our entire lives away, never knowing and never wondering why we came to be here, in our particular circumstances.

It became impossible for me to move forward spiritually, or in any other aspect of life without answering that question. My journey began many years ago with an experience which was pivotal in changing the direction of my life.

In my early twenties, after having studied dreams for several years, I had barely cracked the surface of my spiritual search for truth. I still had one foot in a life where I scattered my energies at social events with people who didn't share my vision.

One morning, at approximately 1:30 a.m., after attending a party with a couple of female friends, we returned home in a taxi. The driver was a man who immediately intrigued me. He instantly engaged one of my friends, Kim, in a conversation about amateur skating, a sport in which she was a competitor

Dream Yourself Awake

and quite knowledgeable. He seemed to know as much or more than she did, rhyming off names, dates and an extensive list of information on the sport.

As we drove along, I remained quiet and removed from the conversation, gazing dreamily out the window into the evening mist. Eventually we arrived at our destination where my friends exited the cab. As I prepared to follow, the driver peered at me in the rearview mirror, his face dimly illuminated by the lights of the street lamps and the car's interior.

"Why are men afraid of powerful women?" he asked.

I hesitated, then stepped out of the cab into the damp evening air without replying, somehow stunned and mystified by his unusual question.

Months and even years later, as the experience began to filter into my conscious awareness, I realized the driver had been one in a line of spiritual guides I had been working with who are capable of teaching through dreams and on the inner planes. This time he came in a physical experience, in the guise of a taxi driver.

Through time, the question, "Why are men afraid of powerful woman?" slowly grew into a great force within me. At times, a male friend would say, "Don't look at me, there's something powerful in your eyes." I remembered the question and wondered, "What is this power?"

It was a long life pause between that question and the full understanding of its implications. During that period I became more and more interested in the study of dreams. Each night I recorded the events and subjects that were presented. I began to see that my dreams were related to my life and in fact were revealing recurring themes and lessons.

As I began sifting through the raw materials of images and

feelings, a map began to emerge, the way a holograph reveals its true contents when observed correctly. The map was the blueprint leading to my purpose as Soul. It shone through the entanglement of voices, chaos and confusion pointing to a shining destiny of spiritual wealth.

More than anything else I wanted to know this purpose. I followed this map with the greatest of conviction. I saw the truth that was contained in the patterns of everyday life and sought to live from that high place.

The question of the cab driver became the tiny grain of sand placed in the oyster shell of my consciousness. I struggled to force it out, to cover it over, not knowing that it would eventually become a great pearl of wisdom and discovery.

Fifteen years later, I was confronted with a pivotal dream. The events that occurred that night in my inner world set in motion a series of events in my outer life, that immediately began to alchemize raw materials into spiritual gold.

In the dream, there is a circle of geese spinning at a great rate of speed close to the earth. My spiritual teacher and dream guide named Z appears and selects one goose from the circle. He then pulls a feather from the goose's throat.

Unlike other dreams I'd had, the circle of geese began a cycle of healing by unlocking the seal on some ancient tomb of past-life memories. Almost immediately I discovered a subtle energy pulsating around my neck, at first barely tangible, then more and more acutely as if a metal band was strapped around it and growing tighter. This sensation intensified until it became unbearable.

The pressure came with a whole list of other symptoms,

including constant nagging headaches, feelings of isolation, a creative block and severe depression. I attempted to unravel the meaning of the dream, feeling certain that doing so would unlock some important secrets and perhaps give relief to my continuing symptoms.

This was the wind of change blowing me in a new direction. In time the greater vision of Spirit would be realized.

Every child is an artist. The problem is how to remain an artist once he grows up.

Pablo Picasso

Waking Up to the Past

Concealed within our childhood dreams and wishes are the golden seeds of our destiny. These dreams are the back lighting illuminating our inner pathway home to God. Dreams represent a constant vein of truth, woven through lifetimes of Soul's quest for spiritual greatness. Dreams transcend time, personalities and religions.

And dreams tell a story about Soul's everlasting wish to journey back home to God.

I recall my longing for truth as a child and I remember seeking out stories that would remind me of who I was and what my mission was. When I found a favourite story, I would read and reread it often so that I could find that feeling of connection to God that it brought to me.

I spent many hours in the school library in a feeling of meditation waiting to find just the right book that would be the passkey through the doors of my imagination to that evening's voyage. Through these journeys I would explore real places in my inner world of Soul.

Dream Yourself Awake

In class, words became the pallet of my composition and I freely splashed the images across pages. I was the Van Gogh of words with a great reservoir of creativity and enthusiasm.

There weren't many other things in my life that brought that kind of joy. After the circle of geese, this creativity came to a sudden halt. Even my attempts at reading failed as the words seemed to scramble as I searched the page. My concerted effort to focus left me even more frustrated and disoriented.

I became frightened by what was happening and felt at a loss to describe the scope of it to anyone, even close friends. As if looking through a backward telescope life seemed out of reach. The inner voice that had been so familiar as a companion was absent.

When reading becomes a way to numb our creative expression then much of the value of that reading is lost in the effort. I struggled for release from the dismal tomb. Through a small crack in my dungeon wall a light broke through, granting insight into my lost world.

In one dream I am married to a man of nobility whom I love deeply. Our relationship is somewhat of a story in itself and has all the makings of a classic love novel.

The time appears to be in the 1600s in Europe. I am lying on a settee in a sitting room where my husband sits talking with a close friend. They are discussing me. I am very delicate and rely on my husband totally.

At one point I approach my husband to ask, "May I write a book?"

He replies in the manner I expect and accept, "Of course not," he says. I wanted his love more than anything else and so I accepted his answer without debate.

This dream was a window into a past life, and spoke of a silent agreement between my spouse and me. It was the contract we had made as Soul before that lifetime began. I would provide him with beauty and companionship and in return, he would provide me with security and a reprieve from the loneliness endured for a succession of lives.

But, when the clock struck twelve, the dream told me, in some future life I would be required to repay the debt incurred – the price of the choice I made to hold back my Spirit.

The dream of the circle of geese tripped an inner mechanism engaging the forces of cause and effect. The exacting payment for that long ago choice was my current intense struggle to reopen the creative channels that were within me.

I often felt confused about who I was and what I should do with my life. This lack of inner direction was due to my choice to close off the flow of Spirit in order to accommodate my desire for security and comfort.

But I was not allowed to forget my goal of going home to God. Dreams open a door through time and let Soul see its greater destiny beyond karma and reincarnation. Once we catch a glimpse of the true worlds of light and sound, we become like the Hound of Heaven.

When we have earned the right to know our mission, Spirit begins to clear away the illusion of what we've pretended to be and lets us glimpse Soul's greater vision for itself.

The law of growth drives Soul on. We come to these crossroads again and again. Will we choose the road to God or spiritual stagnation?

  Dream Yourself Awake

When the Soul wishes to experience something she
throws an image of the experience out before her
and enters into her own image.

Meister Eckhart

The Eastern Parasite

After the dream of the circle of geese, a subtle, long term restructuring began to take place within me. My attempts to uncover the meaning of the dream all led to dead ends.

I was still plagued with headaches, strange throat symptoms and creative deadlock. In desperation, I asked for a dream answer.

That night, I found myself in a Chinese herbal store. I approached the counter and asked the attendant if she could tell what was wrong with me. She answered, "You have an Eastern Parasite."

The strange spiritual ailment now had a name. The ways this "Eastern Parasite" had dominated the circumstances of my life was complex and confusing. What a parasite does best is embed itself into the deep reaches of the body or mind sometimes causing fatal injury. The paralyzing symptoms were a constant motivation to learn more, in hope that one day I might be free of them.

I began to consider the Eastern culture as a source of answers that might lead to solving the riddle of the parasite's purpose.

Later, another dream showed me the personality and motives of the Eastern Parasite.

I enter a Chinese restaurant where a couple has returned from New York City and ordered a meal. I sit at their table, and because of my limited funds I order the Fortune Cookie Special, that costs only $1.99.

I call the waitress but she ignores me. Again I call but she pretends that I'm not there. I become more assertive and raise my voice to demand that she bring my order. She responds by saying she will take my food to the parking lot. I say firmly, "You must serve me, it's your job."

She responds, "I can't serve you, it's twenty-five years of tradition."

This was the first in a series of dreams all starring this waitress. She would later appear in many different disguises as I learned of the complex hold she had on my life. The dream exposed the presence of some deeply embedded patterns of social conditioning as represented by the ancient culture in which she was born.

In her obstinate stance was the dream's portrayal of the parasite's function: To oppose my good. This was my battle ground to gain control of the inner forces which were so vehemently stationed in opposition of my good, joy, success and abundance.

New York, a famous world destination, is a centre of creative expression, abundance and dreams. The returning couple represents Soul having achieved wholeness, inner union and self-realization.

The parasite in the form of the waitress represents certain narrow and rigid beliefs that are blocking my capacity to receive the blessings that should have accompanied this wholeness. My job was to learn the art of moving through the door of wholeness where the true nature of Soul exists.

The Fortune Cookie Special, a seemingly minor detail of the dream, was actually the focal point of my future healing journey. Dreams often use the double meaning of words to draw parallels between cause and effect as was the case with the fortune-cookie special.

The word "Fortune," related to superstitious beliefs and their link to financial difficulties.

The dream brought to my attention an overriding and recurring lesson that had followed me from lifetime to lifetime. In her way the waitress was daring me to break an old cycle of subservience that had been working against my betterment.

Although this dream was rich in meaning, it was only a link in a long series of inner and outer experiences which would begin to shape my viewpoint.

I began to discover that just as any parasite lives off a weakened host, this parasite had a purpose in keeping me in a state of physical and spiritual poverty. It was sustained by a set of attitudes and social conditions that drained away my creative energy. As long as the parasite kept me unaware of its presence by hiding in the details of my life, it supported itself by creating conditions from which it could feed.

"The events in our lives happen in a sequence in time, but in their significance to ourselves, they find their own order: the continuous thread of revelation."

Eudora Welty

——————— A Clue from the Past

As I began the journey of facing life, it was much like the peeling of an onion. Layer upon layer of dead images had to be examined and let go. I was led to the holistic healing profession in order to understand the causes behind my symptoms and to further my education.

In the first months after my dream of the circle of geese I visited a health practitioner who practised subtle energy work. In observing the tendons on opposite sides of my neck, she noticed their thick sinewy appearance. She said that this was a signal that some traumatic memory was being held in my body. Explaining that this thickening could be compared with the way one could ascertain the age of tree, she was able to tell me that the underlying issues were approximately twenty-five years old.

The phrase twenty-five years struck an image of the recent dream about the waitress. As I began to examine my life twenty-five years before as a ten-year-old, I recalled that it had been an especially difficult period. I was in Grade six and had suffered from the malicious treatment of my teacher.

                     Dream Yourself Awake

I had been accelerated a grade and was a year younger than most of the other children. Looking back, it would seem that a teacher receiving a gifted child into his class would have wanted to nurture those abilities, but it was the exact opposite. I was treated as an outcast and fool by my teacher, Mr. Ulman.

Mr. Ulman's strange teaching style resembled something of a Hitler in that he would separate the students into two groups. Those who qualified to receive good treatment because they met his standards of intelligence, good looks and approval, and those who didn't.

Occasionally he would send the rejects to pick up garbage in the school yard, while the chosen few stayed inside to do art.

One particular episode stood out over all. The entire class was invited to participate in a play. For some reason Mr. Ulman decided to exclude only me out of the whole class of approximately thirty children. Although I was terribly intimidated by this tall and aggressive man, I summoned my courage and asked if I could take part in the play.

In the fashion befitting his tyrannical nature, I became victim of a scheme to weed me out of the running. In an on-the-spot audition, he challenged me to scream in order to qualify for a place alongside my classmates. A simple enough task for any other person in the room.

Standing there, staring up at Mr. Ulman who towered some foot and a half taller than me, I was mortified by the absence of sound from my lips. Subsequently, I was left out of the play.

The whole season of observing my classmates rehearse for the play, plan their costumes and perform was a crushing experience of disappointment. Somehow I made it through that year and moved on with my life. Without the spiritual tools which would have helped me to see the deep lessons in this

Darlene Montgomery

experience, I simply continued on as best I could.

At this much later date and with the new information I'd received through my recent explorations, I was compelled to look for the deeper reasons for such a troubling school life.

The following dream tells of where the karmic patterns had begun.

I am a female teacher in Ireland in the 1700s. I have little if any compassion for the children, in fact my form of discipline is quite brutal. I use the strap generously to enforce my classroom sovereignty.

The karmic residue from this precious life left me with a deep aversion to teaching and discipline. Many of the lessons surrounding discipline began in childhood where I faced harsh, sometimes severe punishment often for minor infractions.

In this present life as I began to explore my skills as a music teacher, I hesitated to use any form of discipline at all. My students often appeared deaf to my instructions.

This occurred so frequently that I decided to observe the ways of teachers who could artfully command the attention of their students. What did they know that I didn't? I spent over 15 years discovering the cause of this spiritual condition, learning and relearning the fine art of discipline combined with love.

On one occasion as I handed out instruments to a group of students, I created havoc by asking the group of primary children which instrument they preferred. From the back of the classroom a teacher said, "There is a time to be nice and this isn't one of them." I began to understand the methods that would provide structure in the learning environment and help me to become a more effective teacher.

                                    Dream Yourself Awake

The connection between this experience and the dream of the waitress was in learning to ask for what I needed to move forward spiritually, and then to exert my voice and will to break free of control and power.

Soul is not a creature of fear and passivity but one of nobility, strength and love.

All of these lessons of self-expression, inner and outer discipline and self-love had been hidden in the folds of the fabric of my life.

Through the dream of the circle of geese, I was now beginning to confront all of the fears that had so far prevented me from living to the fullest.

Ultimately, it is not our credentials but our commitment to a higher purpose that creates our effectiveness in the world.

Marianne Williamson

———— The Messengers of Life

Often in an attempt to awaken us, Spirit will guide us to experiences which remind us of some of our forgotten agreements, made before this life began.

One such incident occurred after my marriage broke down, some seven years before the dream of the circle of geese.

I had taken a position that allowed me plenty of time for extra activities. During that period I took English courses through correspondence as a way to upgrade my education. One assignment required that I write a composition in any style I desired. For a lark, I feigned an attempt at a Shakespearian piece.

Each lesson required mailing to a teacher, so that all correspondence was done by a series of notes made on the pages. As the lessons were returned, I began to take notice of red notations on the pages. "Is this yours?", "Whose is this?" and other curious remarks were becoming common place.

I was oblivious as to what this could mean until, when my Shakespearian piece was returned, I found the page marked with large red letters. The words said, "Please Do Not Plagiarize."

Flabbergasted by the remark, I immediately returned a note explaining that the story along with the rest of the work had been my own. A note came back explaining her perplexity at receiving my work. Its unusual nature amongst the material she had become conditioned to expect, had caught her off guard.

Life continued on and I soon forgot about the incident until the dream of the circle of geese made me look more deeply at the connections in my life. Somehow this event had more meaning than I had originally determined. Could it have been a reminder from Spirit to rediscover my true purpose?

Life's messengers come to us in the form of teachers, friends, movies, books and everything that strikes at the armour of our mind. If we look to the themes as they unravel in our lives, the people who recognize and remind us of certain qualities lying latent inside us, and the images that stir our hearts, we begin to piece together our mission in this life.

Darlene Montgomery

Help thy brother's boat across and lo!
Thine own has reached the shore.

Hindu Proverb

A Theme is Revealed

On a Saturday in the fall of 1993, I was invited to a seminar located in Owen Sound, Ontario. As the featured guest speaker, I was scheduled last on a list of several speakers and performers.

As the afternoon progressed, the familiar tightening began to settle around my throat. As if that weren't enough, a deep and gripping terror followed in close sequence. An overwhelming urgency compelled me to plan ways of escaping from the room.

Finally, I retreated outside in hopes that the cool northern air might bring back my composure. But alas, my feelings of terror continued to escalate. I became very doubtful that I could present a coherent speech for I couldn't collect my thoughts enough to focus on a single idea.

After returning to my seat, I found a workshop was in progress. One of the facilitators, a therapist, was in the midst of a discussion about the healing process and the importance of allowing ourselves the opportunity to grieve our losses.

She spoke about a young man whom she had been treating for depression. Even after being prescribed antidepressants by his doctor he denied anything was amiss. This type of denial was preventing him from taking further steps in his healing process.

As she said the words, "healing our losses," a bell rang somewhere deep inside me. Like a dying woman, images began to flash before my inner screen. I saw the scenes and events of my current life that had spurred me to creative action. There had been certain movies, books and people that reminded me of some promise I had made to myself. I saw an agreement I had made to keep my heart open to my dreams in this life, to remember my purpose and above all else, to stay on track.

As I pieced together my story that day, I looked over the movies and books that had stirred my heart. One such movie was, "Field of Dreams."

At the onset of the story, a farmer named Ray Kinsella hears a voice in his cornfield telling him to, "Ease his pain."

Later, the same voice says, "If you build it, he will come." Ray realizes that he must mow down his corn and build a baseball field. As the story progresses, Ray is prompted to follow his inner voice even when on the brink of financial ruin.

The movie plays itself out where heaven and earth meet on a baseball field. Ultimately, following his own dreams leads him through a sequence of events connecting several others who have been prevented from fulfilling dreams of their own.

As I watched the film over and over again, I was reawakened to a similar theme in my own life whereby my own unfulfilled dreams of many lifetimes were resurfacing.

Another film which came to mind was, "Thunderheart," a story of a man who rejected his roots as an American Indian. A member of the FBI, Ray Levoi, is assigned to help settle a dispute on an Indian reservation. As the story unwinds, Ray begins to have visions of a previous lifetime as the warrior,

Darlene Montgomery

"Thunderheart".

In one vision Ray experiences himself as Thunderheart who is shot in the back while escaping from the U.S. Cavalry.

A relationship develops between him and the local chief, who plays a role in awakening Ray to his real identity. In a particularly compelling scene, the chief reminds Ray of his spiritual destiny when he says, "The blood of Thunderheart runs through your heart like the buffalo. Run to the stronghold, Thunderheart. Run to the stronghold."

Each time I watched this scene, tears would well up in my eyes as the chief spoke. Thunderheart has returned to the location of a recent life where he must face and conquer his fears by confronting those who had caused the deaths of his people and himself. As his heart heals so returns his passion for life.

Therein lay the seeds of my story that day.

I gave my talk that afternoon, while those around me remained unaware of the painful and frightening journey I'd taken inside myself to give it.

As I spoke, I experienced a deepening of my own relationship to a purpose I had forgotten until now. Portraying the truth and telling the stories from within the deep well of my own experiences had released me from a prison of doubt and creative deadlock.

Dream Yourself Awake

"A key element of the Success Process is building relationships with people who care about you and believe in your goals as you grow and expand the possibilities for your life."

~ Stedman Graham

My Agreement

In the book, *Journey of Souls*, by Michael Newton Ph.D., he records experiences of individuals under hypnosis. He is able to take them into the place where they view their past lives and the lessons learned. In this place they plan their future life with others in their Soul group who will incarnate with them to gather experience.

It is explained that these Souls make agreements or arrangements, before entering a lifetime, to have certain experiences and to be party to the needed lessons of each. It is prearranged and mutually agreed that these Souls will learn invaluable lessons together.

I learned that my agreement was to start to be responsible for my own power and with that my own dreams. One of the deepest patterns of my life had been that of living vicariously through others in order to avoid accepting my own power.

For one year I dated a man I'll call Sean. The instant I laid eyes on him I was overwhelmed by an intense familiarity.

After we began dating I found it excruciating to be apart

from Sean. I often fell into deep anguish and loneliness when he didn't call right away.

I was compelled to ask spirit for a dream to explain the reasons for my anxiety.

In the dream the time period is the 1600s in North America. I am being placed in a horse-drawn cart to be taken to jail, accused of being a witch. As the door shuts behind me in the cold, damp, evening air, I recognize Sean though his appearance doesn't resemble the Sean of present life.

The dream seems to say that we are not married but a relationship of some kind has drawn us together. Now we are to part for the last time in that life as I head off to my death.

This dream began to roll back the curtain between the past and the present. The theme of the witchhunts crept into my consciousness over the next months by programs on TV and other avenues. I was haunted and intrigued by the theme as it continued to find its way into my awareness.

Through these methods, my inner guide was helping to free me of the symptoms of fear, mistrust and self-loathing which had been carried forward after this experience.

The separation anxiety didn't immediately disappear after the dream. I would have to face the fear over and over again before it began to loosen its hold on me.

Insight into the pain in my throat came one evening many months later. Sean and I were spending time at his apartment when he reached to pull down a blind and said, "You were killed by a guillotine in a past life."

This Golden Tongued Wisdom is one of the ways Spirit uses another person to convey a message or idea. Individuals to whom

  Dream Yourself Awake

this happens often are oblivious about what they have said.

Future dreams unravelled my history as a supposed witch, and revealed that Sean and others had been drawn into the line of fire, to be outcast and ostracized.

In the not to distant past commonplace vocations such as midwifery, herbalism and even writing, might have given rise to superstition resulting in a woman's execution as a witch.

As time went by, I began to have dreams warning me to move out of my relationship with Sean.

My consciousness became a battleground as I tried to resist what my inner voice was telling me. I was extremely attached to Sean and so much so that I had to break it off numerous times. Each time a strong force would pull us back together. I was warned by Spirit of the faltering of my spiritual growth should I delay too long in leaving.

I finally gathered enough strength to end it. After weeks of grappling with reasons to go back I asked for help from my dreams.

That night I dreamt I was on a subway train in Sean's home country. I exited the train at the end of the line and looked out at a field that I must cross to get to a gate at the other end. As I began to cross, I turned to see a German Shepherd pursuing me along the subway tracks. I run, barely keeping ahead of him as he nips at my heels.

As if in a subtitle for a movie, a statement runs across the screen of my dream saying, "This dog was compelled by Spirit to let you go."

I had recently learned that German Shepherds were my personal dream symbol for men, as in "Germ of Man" or "Seed of Man." This dream helped me to see that Sean was fulfilling an agreement he had made with me as soul, which was not to impede my journey to God in this life.

*To accept the responsibility of being a child of God is
to accept the best that life has to offer you.*

~ Stella Terrill Mann

Expect The Best

We all have those in our lives who act as guides to lend a
hand or to go before and place anchors for the journey ahead.
Our bonds of love create chords of inner communication capable
of crossing long distances.

One summer, a girlfriend of mine, Paule flew to Paris to
attend a spiritual conference. I had wished to go along knowing
that this seminar promised to contain many important tools for
spiritual unfoldment.

Although my plans fell through, Paule came to me in a
dream that weekend and shared a gift in the form of message.
The simple motto she shared through the inner channels was,
"Expect the Best." This statement became the cornerstone from
which I would build a new life.

On many occasions this term would appear to alert me to a
new and better direction by appearing on billboards, television
commercials or in variations of the similar message.

Whenever I became sidetracked into situations that failed to
meet the standards of this motto, I would see some variation of

those key words spelled out in a detracting manner.

With the theme, "Expect the Best", appearing everywhere around me, I was continuously warned by spirit to stay clear of anything or anyone that would take me from my assigned path.

I had recently became involved with a new man. One evening, he and I stood hugging in the living room of his home, I looked over his shoulder at the television that was on with the sound muted. Two words flashed for a moment on the screen which shattered any illusions I might have had about the relationship. They said, "Expect Less."

This awakening alerted me to the fact that I would be selling myself short if I stayed, for this relationship did not meet the standards I was now coming to realize I was worth.

After several weeks, I was quite despondent for no apparent reason. I sat on the edge of my bed going back to a few weeks before when I was buoyant, happy and full of zeal. Suddenly it dawned on me that I might have unconsciously been taking on his grief brought about by the recent separation from his wife.

I began to sing to myself the words, "I return with love that which is not mine. I return with love that which is not mine."

A friend had taught me this phrase which apparently had the power to deflect energies of an unwanted nature. Immediately, I began to feel my energy return as if an eagle within had spread its great wings, ready for flight.

The next evening I went to visit the man I had been seeing. Upon entering the house, I found him and his children depressed and one of them crying.

This confirmed my suspicions that I had been a sponge to the deep emotions of the recent separation. I realized we had been unconsciously attracted to each other to facilitate our lessons: Mine to learn to let go of a pattern of care taking and his to learn to be responsible for his feelings.

Soon after leaving the relationship, I found my energy returning and with it my enthusiasm for life. This lesson would occur many times as I learned to value my own energy and use it wisely.

Upon arriving home one afternoon soon after, I noticed an advertisement in bold blue and white print laying on my doorstep which said, "Expect the Best, We Guarantee It." I picked it up and took it inside to place it on my wall as a reminder of the divine Spirit's promise to me.

What a wonderful life I've had!
I only wish I'd realized it sooner.

~ Colette (1873-1954),
French writer

The Only Way Out is Through

Our dreams can call forth enough power to burst the bonds that have kept us imprisoned for lifetimes. We can be shocked into an awareness that what we have been living is an illusion far from our true mission. Then we must be led, step by step, back to the truth of who we are.

After my dream of the geese, I became aware of a feeling behind me, a terrible lifelike energy as if someone were choking me. All my attempts to discover its identity left me with the same frustration and sense of isolation.

A friend, Graig, agreed to exchange treatments in the healing modalities in which we each were trained. I was trained in Educational Kinesiology™, a system which balances the dimensions of the brain. He was trained in Structural Integration™, a system which assists the release of deeply-held patterns within the body.

In both of these healing systems we learn to translate the unconscious ways we hold our bodies into clear messages about our beliefs.

Graig encouraged me find the position which best emulated the struggle I was under and to describe what I was experiencing. Observing me, he suggested that I gave the appearance of sitting inside something like a box. I too felt a distinct impression of being imprisoned within a structure.

That night I was shown from a higher viewpoint what that box-like structure contained.

In the dream I am the daughter of a poor black mother. I have to sing to support my family. Somehow I meet a wonderful man and I envision the life of joy and wealth we will have for he has a wealthy family. Behind me I become aware of a sister. She is crying because she knows she will not have the life I will have.

In this dream, the sister was the Eastern Parasite, the part of myself that had been behind me, choking my potential. She existed through sustaining her own holographic universe that contained all of the conditions that were now plaguing me.

That universe was dependent on my agreement with the beliefs and attitudes of that place. These included a poverty consciousness, unhappy relationships and all of the natural limitations of those beliefs and attitudes.

The dream points to a series of lifetimes following in succession where music was linked to poverty. The persona of starving artist or musician had become so familiar that in this life I put it on as if it were a pair of worn, comfortable shoes. My present profession of musician had yielded me only the most meagre income so that I was constantly in fear of survival. The familiar world governed by the sister as the Eastern Parasite was what I was now fighting so hard to free myself from.

She was carrying on the duty of providing for me as Soul.

Her love and caring had become a suit of armour that now encumbered my journey. I had reached a crossroad in my awareness where I no longer needed to identify with such limitations.

I had expanded my viewpoint to see possibilities that existed outside of her state of consciousness.

She was only as real as the energy that she could sustain through my permission. The inner marriage that the dream promised was still only a possibility until I could take possession and accept that reality as mine.

Life is the childhood of our immortality.

~ John W. von Goethe

Making Sense of History

One evening I was invited to join two friends at the theatre to watch *Sense and Sensibilities*. Unaware of what this invitation would invoke, I became entranced by the unfolding tapestry of rich plots and scenery in the movie.

As if in a dream which frames all the contents of the dreamer's most pertinent lessons, films can bridge the unconscious gap between our past and our present. A movie can be a trigger for a deeper awareness of ourselves and of characters we have played. And such was the case for me.

Sense and Sensibilities centered around a wealthy family of nobles in England in the 1800s. They were confronted with the sudden loss of the father. As was customary, the son inherited the estate and family fortune. The mother and three daughters were now at the mercy of his whims.

In spite of the father's last request that the son look after his mother and sisters, greed soon takes over and he offers only a meagre allowance. The women have no choice but to accept an offer from a great-uncle to live on his estate in a dilapidated cottage in the country.

The women are thrust far down the rung of fortune they had known. The mother is now duty bound to see that each of her daughters finds a partner in marriage to ensure some kind of future security for them and herself.

A woman's education often focused on the cultivation of qualities that made her a good candidate for marriage. It was to a mother's advantage to ensure her daughters would marry well.

The film depicts some of the suitable occupations for women like singing, music or poetry. Writing or more intellectual pursuits were frowned upon.

Each of the three sisters must face the test of falling into society's rules or to transcend the limitations of her circumstances.

This timely film shone a light upon the root causes of my recent creative deadlock. My association with music over many lifetimes was the social leavener and panacea, which had afforded me certain freedoms and opportunities.

The following dream opens the door for more understanding around music and the Eastern Parasite's role.

I am at a table in a restaurant with my husband. I have a musical instrument which is in pieces on the table. A Chinese waitress comes to serve us. She has a degree in music. After leaving the restaurant, I am arrested by a policewoman. I question her and learn my husband was behind the arrest. I run home and ask him why he has done this. He says it was to get me off drugs.

The drugs are referring to my dependence on music, degrees and position as a false sense of self. The policewoman represents the feminine aspect of myself whose growth had been arrested. The young Chinese waitress is yet another form of the Eastern Parasite. Her role of servitude, despite her degree in music represents again how the parasite is sustained by outdated traditions. This time it is related to both intellectual pursuits and education.

This next dream let me know that I was on the right track. It was a healing dream that gave the deeper nature of this spiritual lesson.

The setting is a university where I'm waiting in line to pay my tuition. A sign is posted showing the cost of tuition to be $5,000,000. I am uncomfortable when I realize that others in line have no problem with paying the amount. From across the room a sage-like oriental woman comes toward me. An atmosphere of freedom surrounds her. In her hand is a one hundred dollar bill which she places in my hand.

Her offering is symbolic of newly-earned freedom and spiritual wealth. This dream tells how an overemphasis on education places a weight on Soul and is a misplaced attempt to keep an individual from pursuing the true desires of her heart.

As an example of how this can occur, I had a brief experience on a jobsite. I worked in a factory which dispensed sheet music and musical instruments. The space was dark and dreary and many of those employed seemed to have given up on their dreams.

I took the time to ask questions on my breaks and discovered that almost every employee had a degree in music. It became apparent that in most cases they had settled for a steady paycheque rather than risk their lot in the world doing what their heart desired.

At the time I was struggling with my own lack of musical education as I was trying to venture out as a musician. Despite discouragement by many, I gathered my courage to seek out a living through music. Although there wasn't always a steady paycheque I felt I was following the call of Soul.

Later, I saw that through this incident Spirit was providing me with a reflection of my own dead past. Everything about the place spoke of the ending of that history, from the stacks of sheet music, some of them so dated the wrapping would crumble in your hand, to the dark, dreary, surroundings and lifeless faces.

I felt an urgency to clear away much of the useless stock and made it a short term mission to throw stacks of it into a garbage bin.

Although my degrees hadn't been earned in this present life, the memory and attachment to them was at the root of my strong urge to pursue a career in music. In many of those lives I had enjoyed the recognition and prestige that accompanies such a career.

God doesn't care about the personality but only that we find our way back home to It. We must let go of anything that would hold us back from fulfilling our true purpose as Soul.

He who cannot forgive others breaks the bridge over which he must pass himself.

~ George Herbert

Breaking With Tradition

The lesson of twenty five years of tradition that began with the dream of the waitress who refused to serve me had a multifaceted influence on my everyday existence.

The tradition that had been such a strong force in controlling my reality stemmed from the overuse of submission and inaction in successive lifetimes. I had entered this life as an extremely shy person but later somehow emerged with a lion's roar that surprised even me.

Several times over the years, I had been placed in situations where to grow spiritually required me to fight or respond to an aggressor. Each time I was given the opportunity to break the cycle of passivity.

I was shown through dreams just how critical it was for me to release this established role I'd been playing.

Queen Elizabeth and her entourage have driven into a lake with their car. No one is attempting to help because royal etiquette requires a certain conduct of restraint. Queen Elizabeth must pull

herself out of the lake on her own. I go to her later with reverence and give her my regards.

The Queen was a representation of a sovereign rule or set of fundamental laws which had dictated my perceptions and subsequently my actions or lack of actions. The Queen (myself), must take some action or suffer the fate of drowning in outdated traditions. The circumstances of life were compelling me to learn the art of survival in spite of inborn constitutional restrictions.

The Queen was enslaved by the same constitutional order she governed. This translated into a submissive or passive behaviour born out of the generations and lifetimes of training.

In order to loosen the hold of these influences I was taken through a series of dreams and outer lessons to both encourage and teach me. I saw the many lives I had spent playing characters of nobility without any real influence or power.

The following dream shows how this played out.

An Indian woman of position has a gold chain denoting her status. It is very valuable but she owns nothing else. The chain is an integral part of her family tradition, which has been passed down through generations. It is worthless because she remains a prisoner of the hierarchy she is in.

The dream showed yet another face of the same problem. In this dream I am the woman, bound by her position as a noblewoman and devoid of the freedom typically associated with wealth. The culture had automatically assigned her to a hierarchy where she had little choice to determine her future.

I was discovering something about inherited unconscious

  Dream Yourself Awake

values. My own reluctance or lack of drive to have money stemmed from past lives where societal structures had bound me into positions of status.

Now Soul's desire to break free of the restrictions of the past was straining at the doors of my heart.

We are all called to live with integrity, to express the truth as we perceive it, and to trust God's ability to use what we offer.

~ Elizabeth J. Canham

_____ Something Borrowed

The theme of "Expect the Best" continued to wind its way through the fabric of my life. In my attempt to end an old cycle I was encountering large amounts of resistance. As in the nature of cycles, they normally dip low before going high.

In changing my patterns I came upon a wall of resistance so dense, I sincerely wondered if I would succumb to the past. One important dream foretold a new perspective on my self image in the area of roles.

I am working for a large corporation as a maid. I am in the CEO's office, where at a table is laid an array of gourmet foods. He orders me to sit down and eat, but I feel unworthy and embarrassed by this rich display. He insists I eat, so I sit down at the table. At that moment an old boyfriend enters the room. He is also employed by the company as an executive and wonders at my presence at the table. He argues against allowing me to eat the fine food, however the CEO insists that I stay and eat.

The test of the dream was in whether I would succumb to the pressure of outside forces or accept the gifts of consciousness offered by my spiritual guide. The dream further exposed in a dramatic way an ingrained inclination to remain in subordinate roles as seen in the original dream of the Chinese waitress.

The high spiritual aspirations of Soul were reflected in the food while the adverse effect of giving away my power would be a test for me in the human consciousness. The boyfriend represented an ingrained pattern of rigid role-oriented relationships.

I seemed to have had a knack for attracting relationships which made it easy for me to make myself least in importance. My earlier prompting to expect the best nagged at my old state of consciousness, making it uncomfortable to participate in the rigid roles I had easily accepted before.

In order to take the next spiritual step, my entire belief structure would have to be rebuilt from top to bottom. Each time I entertained the idea of staying longer in my self-imposed prison, I was given a sharp reminder through inner dreams and outer waking dreams that it was not to be.

One such dream with a similar theme demonstrates the impossibility of going back to what I was.

I am in a restaurant, sitting at a table next to an oriental woman. She is paying for my meal and is quite wealthy. She orders a bowl of wonton soup but the waiter gives me a knowing look. I acknowledge his look with a smile for we both know that she cannot order wonton soup because this is not a Chinese restaurant.

Looking over at another table I notice a restaurant bill left for

Art Garfunkle, the musician. I realize he had been there before us and think to myself, "Someone famous could eat in a public place and remain inconspicuous."

This dream was the dividing line between past and future. The Chinese woman again was the parasite now in a reversed role, as a wealthy persona. Normally until now she has been the waitress but my inner guide has now taken on this form to force the parasite into a more accurate portrayal of her nature.

By entertaining the idea of an old state of consciousness which had given me certain rewards, I was holding myself back spiritually. The wonton soup was an ironic reference to the Eastern Parasite's diet.

Art Garfunkle represented an artistic past which was no longer a threat to my autonomy. Fear of success had played a part in the poverty brought from lifetimes where knowledge, creativity and influence had led to my untimely death.

This dream was reassuring while at the same time disturbing, for in spite of my growing awareness I found myself wanting to go back to some of the things I had found comforting before this turn of events. Although I had seen clearly the future as it was laid out as a potential reality, I began to feel this struggle would go on indefinitely.

Dream Yourself Awake

There's no higher art than living a good life.

~ Marianne Williamson
A Return to Love

Getting Started

Just as the tide comes in and then moves out, and the seasons come and go, all life, including our individual lives, moves in cycles. The decisions one makes at the end of a cycle determines the path one will walk for a time after that. At the point where one cycle ends and a new one begins we must be mindful of our choices and words.

During a very difficult period of my life I decided to practise the principles of the spiritual law of attitudes by going on a mental fast. I had known through my studies that thoughts create reality and so took the advice of Anthony Robbins from his book *Notes from a Friend*, and started a mental fast. This meant that for ten days I would invest my thoughts and energy consciously toward only positive ideas, goals and attitudes.

I set a date for the fast to begin and on that day began to replace all my thoughts with ones which resonated with the life I desired.

I chose words like peace, contentment, surrender and love and constantly replaced thoughts of fear and doubt with these.

Darlene Montgomery

Almost instantly I found my inner and outer life changing. All of life seemed to mirror the wisdom of the choice I had made. This method of thought replacement was quite different than the affirmations which I had once used. Now I saw my thoughts as a stream constantly flowing by and my job as the conservationist responsible for keeping it flowing with crystal-clear purity.

Immediately new opportunities began to present themselves. Difficulties at home and in relationships began to improve. Others began to notice the change brought about by my new perspective.

Some time later a dream confirmed a bountiful harvest.

A farmer is harvesting a field of grapes. He has developed a hybrid by introducing a new strain of grapes with the original. He calls the new crop, "The Flute of God."

The Flute of God, a book by Paul Twitchell, had laid the foundation for my new perspective. In it he teaches that we, as spiritual beings, are responsible for creating our lives by the thoughts we hold in our minds. He says, "What we hold in our thoughts is bound to manifest in this world."

My dream was telling me that by applying the principles in the book in a correct way I was creating a new hybrid life. With this change, I began to feel a renewed sense of enthusiasm for life.

I had been convinced for many years that there was a special plan for me that included suffering and despair. I saw my dreams as being out of reach and believed on a deep level that I was in the unique class of Souls for whom the normal laws of creation would not work.

The Eastern Parasite was invested in this attitude and was very powerful in making sure that I would remain in a powerless state.

Now in discovering that my thoughts were an important key in resolving the hold of the parasite, I had renewed hope and vitality. Still, the journey was only beginning and many tests were to follow.

Reach high, for stars lie hidden in the Soul.
Dream deep, for every dream precedes the goal.

~ Pamela Vaull Starr

When Laws Change

There is never a straight path to any goal. We are forever learning and relearning the same principles in evermore complex patterns. At the foundation of life are the same immutable laws of the universe. These laws are the fabric behind every manifestation in this world.

The law of attitudes comes into play every time we begin to dream, think or imagine anything we wish to have. If held in our imagination long enough these conditions will manifest.

At each level of consciousness these laws operate a little differently. In the physical world, an increased span of time is required to manifest our goals as they are brought through the dense levels of physical matter, while in the higher worlds, where levels of vibration become increasingly fine, thoughts manifest instantly.

From my recent discoveries I had seen that a little bit of discipline could yield an abundance of good. Of course I was only a novice and to maintain this attitude day after day and week after week was the real test.

I had seen the Law of Attitudes at work in my daily life. Next I was introduced to another of the spiritual laws through a dream that contained a riddle.

I had left my car parked in a lot. I see a white car that I recognize as mine but when close up realize it isn't my car at all. I'm suddenly very nervous at the thought that my car is missing and that I have left it so long.

A friend notices another car on a hillside covered in leaves. The bumper is exposed showing it is white like my own. Pushing the leaves off, we see that it is a BMW, apparently left and forgotten by its owners long ago. My friend offers me the keys , saying that I might as well have the car for it appears that no one will return to claim it.

Realizing that it is a "standard," I become nervous about driving one after so long. Getting behind the wheel, I put it in neutral and ease it off the hill. I attempt to start it but it won't start for some reason.

Upon awakening, I saw that the dream was offering a spiritual opportunity to master a state of consciousness embodied in the forgotten vehicle. The BMW, I would discover, represented the state of self-realization or "standard" that must be mastered. The question of "ownership" in the dream is a clue to this mastership.

The keys represent spiritual principles that I have in my possession. They alone are not enough without the awareness of how to integrate those lofty principals into this present reality. One of the ways that we gain self-mastery is in governing this physical reality. As Soul, I had made an agreement to overcome passivity in mastering the physical world.

The abandoned vehicle was the dream censor's way of concealing the full impact of how in some previous lifetime I had forfeited my opportunity to attain Self and God-realization.

I was now entering a cycle which required that I rediscover spiritual skills and abilities abandoned somewhere back on the road to God. I was at a loss to start the car for I had yet to master the state of consciousness, necessary to fully possess the new vehicle.

Several clues were hidden within the dream. The keys to operate in this new consciousness were already in my possession. The car or state of consciousness was also already in my possession even though I often felt that others seemed more deserving. I was the actual owner who had forgotten, not lost the car. Neutrality could begin to move me out of a stuck state of consciousness.

The final ways of mastering that awareness were still to be discovered over the next few years. The BMW is a high performance vehicle and to own one means that one agrees to demonstrate a certain excellence.

Once I learned to shift gears, and could operate easily in that state of consciousness, the vehicle would be mine.

This dream was a doorway offering me entrance to a new life. Unbeknownst to me, the time between this dream and the reality it offered was several years.

"Life is a dream but the dream has become so commonplace that we cannot see it."

~ Heather Hughes-Calero

The Answer at Last

One Saturday in February 1996, I attended a day-long seminar with the theme, "The Sacred Hand of God."

Surprisingly the temperature soared to almost seventy degrees fahrenheit, more than unusual for Toronto in winter. People roamed the streets with shorts and light clothing feeling free and appreciative of the temporary reprieve from cold weather.

Normally, to organize and carry out an event with many speakers and performers meant a day of constant motion accompanied by a high level of stress. On arrival at the hall, I ran about in a frenzy to ensure signs were in place and other variables were in order.

I observed the draining of my energy so early in the day and shifted into a more relaxed perspective. With that came a feeling of peace and surrender I had been without for a long time.

As the day progressed I felt carefree and alive, laughing and listening to the various speakers. I watched with amazement at how the day was unfolding without my interference.

At suppertime, a group of friends joined me at a restaurant where we enjoyed conversation and laughter. Suddenly, I was overcome with a feeling of anxiety much like the one I'd had months before in that small northern town before my speech.

The same caged feeling and terror swept over me. I became overcome with apprehension finally blurting out, "Something is wrong with me and I don't know what."

As I went over in my mind the events that had led up to this moment, it occurred to me that the spiritual currents surrounding the days events may have overloaded me.

Urgently, I asked if we could leave and take a walk outside, hoping that it might help me in some way. As we exited the restaurant, my companions made a quick decision to visit a coffee shop across the street. Following them inside, I reluctantly sat down.

While attempting to relax, my attention was drawn to a tight band of nausea across my abdomen. Abruptly the tension subsided as if an obstruction had suddenly broken free. At that moment I knew the meaning of the dream I'd pondered and struggled to understand for years. The circle of geese, which had inspired so many uncomfortable changes both physical, emotional and spiritual, and that had been so stubborn in its revelation, was suddenly very clear.

The feather in the throat of the goose was a quill, an ancient writing tool.

At the same time, it also occurred to me that the nausea was caused by the urgency of a story which was trying to get through. In the ease of the daily events, I had forgotten that in approximately one hour I was to give a short story to the audience of about two hundred.

In that moment, all of my efforts of the past five years came to a conclusion, for now I saw that writing was the forgotten tool which best allowed me to express my creativity in this life. My mission was to write.

That night, as I sat on stage telling my story, I felt strangely at peace.

*Every blade of grass has its Angel that bends over it
and whispers, "Grow, grow."*

~ The Talmud

Recognizing the Habits

The lesson of accepting God's blessings is often easier said than done. When we accept these blessings, life works like a well-oiled machine. When we set limitations on Spirit we are in a sense saying, "I am more knowledgeable than God."

The idea of accepting goodness in my life brought along a foreboding. My dreams often came to educate me on the strange and subtle ways that the parasite had permeated my lifestyle in order to sustain itself.

An adaptive subordinate role in relationships had me giving all my energy to others. Spending so much time with those who had chaotic lifestyles and emotional habits would subtly drain away my own resources.

One dream showed the irony of this habit.

I am shopping for food in a grocery store with my sister. The cashier punches in the amount of each item including several dozen cucumbers that my sister has selected. The total is more than I have in my wallet and since I am paying I tell her to put all

Dream Yourself Awake

but a few back. Only then do I have the right amount of money to pay the bill.

At the time I was in a relationship which was draining my resources on many levels. My sister as the Eastern Parasite was buying into something I neither needed nor could afford.

The law of economy was being breached every time I compromised my values. Small things, like leaving my own life unattended in order to supply the needs of another was an example of this. By expending so much energy I was depleting my resources and creating an imbalance in my life.

I was making the necessary adjustments in my attitude and outlook thus conserving energy to carry out the actions needed to support myself on all levels.

As I learned to live in harmony with the will of Spirit my dreams began to come to life. I gained new energy and inspiration to write and plan for the new life I had envisioned.

*Man is asked to make of himself what he is supposed
to become to fulfill his destiny.*

~ Paul Tillich

Fear Behind All Fears

It takes great preparation to enter the higher states of consciousness. Each new step requires a series of tests in order to temper the individual for the higher state.

I found myself visiting and revisiting my new life. For a time I would experience a feeling of lightness only to find some situation would plummet me back into a spiritual valley.

I began to recognize that I was being brought back and forth from one reality to another in order that I could become used to the difference between the two. As I became more and more acclimatized to living with greater degrees of freedom, I grew increasingly capable of recognizing the old traps.

Inward preparation through dreams and spiritual exercises was beginning to pay off as I saw the pitfalls of giving power away to people and situations which prevented my full expression as Soul.

I often looked back on the woman who in the past had a high tolerance for inappropriate behaviour, a concept I had read about in Charles Whitfield's book, *Healing the Child Within.*

I could see why all the little steps were so necessary, each shaping my viewpoint and sharpening my awareness for the journey ahead. My old state of consciousness, often symbolized in dreams as the eastern culture, had held me in its grasp for centuries. It had formed a magnetic attraction to poverty and other forms of suffering.

As I entered into my new life, I often experienced resistance at various crossroads, sometimes losing hope. On the day of my first television interview to promote a seminar I was presenting on dreams, I pulled out of the driveway for the one hour trip to the studio.

At first it rained only lightly, but as I drove the rain increased in volume until I was in the midst of a torrential downpour. When the rain moved in, I noticed a mood enveloping me like a thick soup. I strained to gain an awareness into the reasons for it.

I began to suspect negative resistance and so set up a test. Creating an on the spot spiritual exercise, I visualized a large broom sweeping away the rain, while I ordered the negative power to move out of my way.

I said to myself, "If it stops raining by the time I arrive at the studio, I will take it as proof that the rain and mood are meant as resistance to success."

Five minutes later, as I pulled into the driveway of the studio, it had not only stopped raining but the sky was blue and clear. The torpor began to lift as I made my way into the studio. The interview and taping went amazingly well.

I myself do nothing.
The Holy Spirit accomplishes all through me.

~ William Blake

————— Energy Leaks

In order to truly leave behind the old life, I had to be strengthened in several areas. The Eastern Parasite's fodder was made up of a combination of emotional leftovers and its need to foster relationships that supplied them.

Episodes like the following were at the root of my problems. One evening a friend called looking for emotional support. He was only one of several individuals who took advantage of my free counselling sessions. Subsequently, I spent most of two hours on the telephone rescuing this person from his feelings of depression.

After hanging up, I felt that the life force had been drained out of me. I fell into bed and had a dream.

In the dream my friend Paule, who had delivered my earlier dream message, "Expect the Best," appeared to me. She had a plane ticket to travel anywhere in the world and offered me the chance to travel with her. I had been looking after her plants and had allowed a cat to get into them.

She asks, "Why don't you put a screen around them?"

It was obvious to me that I had allowed my valuable energy and new growth to be invaded by someone. By continuing in this helping behaviour, I simply prolonged my own suffering and prevented another from learning responsibility. As we become more committed to our dreams, we learn to allow others to handle their own difficulties.

This was what I came to call an "energy leak".

My capacity for spiritual freedom was greater than what I was allowing myself. By continuing to be a martyr to another's constant woes I was unknowingly breaking a spiritual law of interference. The result was a lessening of the life pulse within me. For the new and fragile growth of my own life force to flourish, I needed to protect myself from intrusion by those who might carelessly trample the energy of my dreams.

The cat was the individual's emotional body as it brought impurities to my garden of truth. The person was harboring attitudes that were damaging to the fresh and natural order of my inner sanctum.

My spiritual contract could be fulfilled only if I left myself with enough fuel for the journey. In order to keep up with the pace I needed my full share of courage, faith and love.

*It is well to understand as early as possible in one's
writing life that there is just one contribution which
every one of us can make; we can give into the
common pool of experience some comprehension of
the world as it looks to each of us.*

~ Dorothea Brande

—————— Between Two Worlds

Stepping out on this new shore, was much like the swimmer gazing into the depths of the unknown ocean. There is a yearning to experience the freedom which comes from leaving the shore while at the same time the imposing height of the waves challenge the approach.

One dream portrayed the deep inner struggle I was having.

I'm with a woman. There are huge crowds of people around us. I'm going to fly up and over them. I tell her that if she's not coming, I'm going without her. At first I don't think I'll be able to get over because the people are standing on each others' shoulders.

We fly higher and higher. People are excited and happy for us. Then at some point the woman meets a black man. I think he's wealthy. I am wealthy in this place too, but I know that in the other world I live in I'm not. The woman is going with him and she is hanging back a bit to be with me but I encourage her to stay with him.

Later there is a huge tornado. The man is on a motorcycle.

The other woman is hanging back and there is a choice to be made; go on and be saved or stay and be killed in the storm.

This dream is a spiritual opportunity for Soul to move forward to greater heights and new lands. The black man is my own spiritual potential possessed with the qualities of strength, wisdom and courage. He holds the passkey that can open the door to freedom.

The conflict between my loyalties to an old dependent self or the potential state that is being offered in this cycle is evident. It is apparent that without making a clear and determined selection I will be thrust into the conditions of chaos and upheaval.

This upheaval arrived each time I faltered in living up to the heights of my inner vision. I was tested each time I attempted to move out of the old into the new. Obstacles were in my path to see if I would have the spiritual fortitude to pursue the dreams of my heart.

It came as the rain that fell on the way to the television studio, the inertia each time I sat down to write and those around that subtly or not so subtly tried to usurp me from fulfilling the potential of my dreams.

I woke up to the realization that others merely reflect various degrees of our own awareness. Many times we are fooled into accepting the limitations of those who have an investment in keeping us as we are.

When conditions in our consciousness change, outer conditions begin to align themselves to reflect the more refined nature of Soul. Relationships that cannot withstand the higher vibrations will naturally fall away.

This principle of growth is demonstrated in the following

dream. It occurred shortly after leaving the last in a series of unsuccessful relationships.

I am living with a Frenchman. We are not married but have enjoyed a frivolous relationship based on convenience. I decide to move out but feel guilty at leaving him behind.

As I walk down the street I am pondering my guilty feelings. Suddenly it dawns on me; I have done the work to grow spiritually and so have earned the right to move on. I feel ecstatic as I realize this new principle.

This dream released me from any guilt associated with past and recent choices to withdraw from relationships that were not benefitting me spiritually.

My reluctance had been due to an unconscious sense of responsibility and resulting guilt for abandoning others to face their tests and lessons alone.

The law of growth requires the continuous advancement of Soul toward God. With this new awareness I was free to continue toward the greater destiny I had seen foreshadowed in my dreams.

*I realized that if I was a prism through which God's
love and light flowed, my obligation was to keep
that prism as clean as possible.*

~ Erin Tierney Kramp

Accentuate the Positive

We are powerstations walking around the planet. Our thoughts generate energy and our feelings can concentrate that energy and send it across the planet to a friend or someone unknown to us.

Many individuals are sensitive to the thoughts and feelings of others. Some even practice being sensitive. For those who are extremely sensitive it is difficult to discern between causes that originate from outside and inside. A constant barrage of free-floating emotional and mental paraphernalia is pulled into their sensitivity field.

Once when a friend came to town to babysit her niece and nephew while her sister was away, she drove to another town on an errand. I had been visiting in their area and was on my way back when I became turned around and lost. I felt an anxiety and confusion that seemed out of context.

Later when I spoke to my friend she told me she had been lost at that exact time. This wasn't the first time I'd experienced this. Sometimes I'd feel such things and suspected the source was external. Then I'd receive a phone call from a friend saying, "I've been thinking about you all day. I'm having a terrible time and need to talk to you."

Those who have practised being open as healers, psychics or prophets in previous lives may have an ingrained memory of this openness as a spiritual lesson for these souls. We hear a lot about psychic protection, protecting your energy field and various systems of a similar nature.

Several years ago I was given a dream which held the solution to many of my problems with sensitivity and energy transference. It wasn't until five years later that I would begin to understand the full scope of its implications.

I am in a Tai Chi class where a woman is the teacher. Someone tells me that when I was pregnant I got cancer. After the class the teacher comes to tell me that in her observations of me I had a positive charge of electricity.

The principles of electricity that the dream referred to held the key to the source of my sensitivity. Tai Chi is the art of balancing the life force or Chi internally in such a way that it creates harmony in body, mind and spirit.

The elements of positive and negative are in all bodies, plants and organic life forms. This dynamic energy that sustains all life must flow freely through the body like a river. There are many streams of energy that regulate our systems. The main dynamic of positive and negative has an interplay within the brain, body and spirit. Originally we are Spirit and consist of one pure stream of light and sound. As Spirit steps down into the psychic worlds it splits into two, positive and negative.

It wasn't until several years later that I fully understood the

Dream Yourself Awake

energy dynamics when I dealt with others. I began to notice something with certain individuals. At times when entering a conversation I would start out with a level of energy. Later I would notice a depletion in my energy similar to a light fading within me.

One afternoon I saw an answer to this dream question in a television show about lightning.

As clouds form high in the atmosphere they are filled with large, fist-sized ice pellets. Smaller pellets rush upward striking the larger ones, building up an electric charge within the cloud. Eventually the cloud reaches its optimum charge and must discharge.

On earth, trees, people or metal poles all emit positive streamers which are like a thread of electricity up into the sky. The cloud releases what is known as a lightning leader. This leader descends toward earth searching for a positive streamer.

After making contact with the streamer, tens of thousands of volts of electricity surge forth until finally the charge is completely depleted. This is how the cycle completes itself.

I began to look at how this might tie in with my own lesson of energy transference which had affected me for so long. Over the next period I began to observe my interactions with others.

Then, on one occasion, I could actually feel my energy draining in an interaction with an individual. This person was nice enough. He was interested in going on a date and had called to make arrangements to meet. As we spoke, I could almost see the degrees of a barometer sliding downward. I took note of it and the next time he called I told him I didn't feel this was going to work for me.

Soon after, I was preparing to give a speech to a group and was searching through my dream journal for examples of my experiences. I opened to a dream which gave me the final piece in the puzzle.

There is an electronic woman. Men are attracted to her because she is electric. Whenever she gets close to anything electrical it discharges onto her.

I was the electronic woman. This positive charge had been an open invitation to anyone who needed to balance their own energy. The imbalance had begun when, as a healer in other lifetimes, I had fallen into using the positive currents rather than the pure spiritual current.

Using positive currents involves a bending of the forces of nature and therefore falls into the arena of magic. When being a channel for the true spiritual current the individual simply lets the will of Spirit be done. He or she does not try to direct Spirit.

This was the real key and the cause of many of my difficulties. As long as I was working in the psychic arena I would be subject to the laws governing it. In later dreams I would find out more about the trap of living in power.

Between living and dreaming there is a third thing.
Guess it.

~ Antonio Machado

The Riddle of Light and Dark

We are often given a course to follow through the inner direction of Spirit.

It may come through a dream that poses a riddle, or theme that must be learned, digested and integrated over time and through many experiences. All of those difficulties that existed in me were tied into some very basic spiritual laws of which I was about to learn more.

The following dream was a spiritual riddle, again around the subject of positive and negative.

I am to spend four months living in the penthouse of an apartment building with a master of an eastern-style religion. I am concerned that we will run short of food and supplies. He says to me that he will teach me how to make the room dark by closing the blinds. I say that I will teach him to make it light by keeping the shutters open.

It took more than four months for me to begin to unravel the many levels of this dream.

Although my inner dream guide provided me with some very strong clues, it wasn't until a year later that the full meaning of the dream became apparent. There was a lengthy series of both inner and outer experiences leading up to my discovery.

The factor of the four-month stay alluded to one of the divisions of the spiritual regions of God known as the mental plane, or the fourth plane by various religions. In the psychic regions, there are a total of five planes which must be mastered. This area is the home of good and evil, dark and light and all factors of polarity.

By playing with the forces of good and evil, positive and negative, I was confined to the psychic regions of heaven.

The master of the Zen religion's presence in my dream pointed to where I had spent numerous lifetimes honing the skills of the mental world. The teachings of Buddha, Confucius and others have their home in this region of the psychic worlds. To stay and play with these forces was the trap.

The common misconception used in many philosophies today is that positive energy can be used to manipulate events in our lives without cost to ourself. I would often use affirmations to conjure up desired outcomes, finding good results over time. This was my introduction into the wonder-workings of the mind powers and their usefulness in my life.

There came a time however when the affirmations abruptly stopped working.

The following dream addressed an over-dependence on my use of affirmations.

A young child has been left on her front porch by her mother. She is wearing a T-shirt with affirmations that are somehow supposed to protect her from harm.

A positive attitude is a start but simply not enough without the appropriate action as the dream shows. We must use the right approach in each of life's circumstances if we are to expect success. The dream master is highlighting how the overuse of affirmations is causing real neglect of the vital issues of life.

This came as a shock at the time, for I thought I had discovered a magic tool for manifesting all my dreams and a way out of all problems.

Instead, by drawing the forces of nature down to answer a request, I had become limited to the worlds of mind. I would stay in this strange borderlike world, a spiritual refugee, until I learned the secret of living in the higher worlds of pure Soul.

*My purpose, as simple as it seemed, was to let God's
love flow through me.*

~ Erin Tierney Kramp

Magic and the Mind

I began to see that the lessons of the present were a continuation of the past. Experimenting with positive thinking was only a rudimentary step on Soul's way home to God. This use of positive energy is an illusive trap which can hook Soul for eons into believing it has achieved a high state of consciousness.

This dream presented the trap of manifesting desires through using willpower or magic.

I am in a friend's house where he is performing a ceremony to conjure up the forces of magic through the use of crystal bowls, each measuring different frequencies of sound. He uses a magic wand and I am fearful of the powers which I feel swirling around me.

Another man comes to me with a wand attempting to use it on me, but I escape out the back door where I meet with a woman whom I know to be wise.

  Dream Yourself Awake

This dream warned me to stay away from tricks of the mind and falling into the use of magic. The man in my dream was someone who had manifested many fine things in a material sense by using positive energy.

At the time of the dream, I was experimenting with ways of manifesting abundance in my life. I was attempting to make the leap from the worlds of mind into the arena of Self-Realization where Soul relies on its own creativity to survive.

Using the psychic tools of the mind was a real attraction because of the familiarity from the lifetimes of use. Secondly, they are more recognizable to the mind which needs complexity to function adequately.

As I struggled to be free of the mind, I faced those situations of the past where I had fallen into the use of power. I was being presented with similar lures and tests.

Ancient superstitions still permeated my consciousness as demonstrated through the magic bowls. To gain entrance into the pure worlds of Soul, means leaving behind the parlour tricks we may have used in our infancy.

This is more easily said than done when faced with prolonged hardship. It is tempting to observe others who seem to amass fortunes as if out of nowhere and think perhaps it would be easier to bend the forces of nature to help Spirit along.

But the will of Spirit can't be bent without causing the user a prolonged stay in the psychic regions.

Soul's single purpose in this life is to come into harmony with Spirit.

~ Rebezar Tarzs

It's Always Darkest

I had understood the hidden meaning of my earlier dream of the circle of geese. This led to an inner awareness of my gift to be a writer.

The next area to clear up was still hovering like a shadowy form below the surface of my awareness. I could still feel the energy looming in my body and experienced degrees of tightness in my throat. But now I had a sense of the journey and that there was a purpose.

One morning I sat in contemplation looking for a sense of inner peace. I felt again this brooding energy. Then I saw or sensed a separate self occupying my inner space. It appeared as an energy, solid as a rock.

It was a self but it wasn't my true self. I now observed it with the eyes of Soul. I saw that it was a creation of pain and anger toward myself and others who had condemned me to die as a witch.

I suddenly felt alone and abandoned by God.

As I looked back on my favourite childhood story titled,

"Little Witch," I saw how at an early age I had already known that I would be unlocking these secrets.

The story is of a young girl named Minx, who lives with her witch mother. Each evening the witch flies out into the evening sky where she casts spells on children turning them into flower pots.

Minx searches through her mother's jars of spells to find a fairy who can turn the flowerpots back into children. And everyday as she brushes her hair, the image of a lovely woman appears in the mirror. As time goes by Minx's love grows for this silent yet hauntingly beautiful woman.

Finally, Minx cannot hold her feelings back any longer and blurts out the words, "I love you." These magic words free the woman from the mirror and a spell placed upon her by the witch many years ago.

Minx discovers that the beautiful woman is her mother who is also a fairy.

My childhood fixation on this story was a foreshadowing of my journey to uncover the hidden part of myself locked away in the mirror of my own consciousness. The witch symbolized the Eastern Parasite and the use of power and magic that had enslaved me. The mother's loss of voice mirrored my own inability to express the truth locked away inside me.

The answer is so neatly tucked away in the story. Freedom comes through love.

Hope is that thing with feathers that perches in the Soul and sings the tune without the words and never stops ... at all.

~ Emily Dickinson

Leaving the Old Life

For several months I lived with a foot in one life and one in the other. I repeatedly glanced into the future while at the same time letting go of the past.

My daily life was filled with new learning as I studied and learned to apply the principles of healing as practitioner of Educational Kinesiology™. I was working on the development of my writing and going through the struggles of inadequacy and acceptance with the help of my editor who nurtured me through times of hardship.

My personal life was at an awkward stage through most of this period primarily due to old feelings of separation. All these details would eventually be sorted out as the presence of the Eastern Parasite transformed me into a stronger and more vital human being.

Understandably, this parasite was not going to let go without a fight. It was a creation and a stubborn one at that.

An important factor in the transition, was my attitude about money. Although money seemed to be a symbol for a higher

Dream Yourself Awake

state of consciousness, it was also a practical barometer for how much I was "accepting the best."

I received an invitation to attend a short seminar on a variety of healing modalities. One of the subjects was Applied Kinesiology™, a methodology used to clear emotional, mental and physical blockages.

During a segment of the course which focused on clearing fears and phobias, the facilitator asked for a volunteer on which to demonstrate a particular technique. I eagerly raised my hand and asked to be cleared of my fear of success for this theme had come into my awareness many times lately.

The facilitator, an older gentleman, was befuddled by the idea that such a fear could exist but my insistence won him over.

As I laid on a table at the front of the room. He asked me to think of success while he tested the endurance of a muscle in my arm (a technique known as muscle testing). When my muscle tested weak, it indicated a weakened energy response to success. He then cleared the blockage by tapping the associated meridians, which are the body's energy wires, until he got a strong response.

After arriving home later that day, I was told I had received a phone call from a relative regarding an inheritance. This confirmed for me that by eliminating these blocks in my subconscious, a clear pathway was opening which would allow greater abundance to enter my life.

It's no use walking anywhere to preach unless our walking is our preaching.

~ St. Francis of Assisi

The Power Within

Our nudges and instincts don't necessarily come in neat, compact installments. At times they may seem to overtake our reasoning. In my life I often felt a deep compulsion to act on these impulses, sometimes at the expense of others.

As years went by I learned to keep my instincts on a leash, realizing that it wasn't necessary to act immediately on my first thought, but instead give myself time to digest and form balanced responses. The following dream foreshadowed my lessons over much of my life to come.

Before me stood two lions at the edge of a cliff. At first I was frightened. I then sang the spiritually-charged word, "Hu" which allowed my heart to fill with love. My fear subsided and I easily approached the lions, even patting them on the head.

Lions are the noble qualities of Soul. Strength, courage and patience were all in my spiritual contract of this lifetime and with it a life lesson of facing the fear of power and leadership.

Dream Yourself Awake

Some time after the dream of the circle of geese, I was studying Educational Kinesiology™ in an attempt to educate myself while at the same time heal some of the difficulties I was having with my throat.

Part of the practise of Edu-K, as it is known, is to put a goal on line by first getting a person to write their goal and then put it into an action that demonstrates how the person would function after having achieved the goal.

Once the goal has been put into the body (much like a programme runs in a computer), then within that frame the person begins to notice where their body, mind or emotions may be acting contrary to the individual's best intentions.

I made a goal of letting the energy flow more easily between my head and my heart while allowing my throat to open in expression.

The dream which came that night demonstrates how I needed to master the powerful flows of energy within my voice.

A woman owns a full grown male lion. She is showing me how to make a sound like the lion and how to train it. She says she can show me in a very short time and that I, too, could befriend the lion. I was uncertain that I could do as she said.

The dream demonstrated that bringing the power of self-expression into balance would be easy through surrendering and accepting my own inner strength. The woman was me in my natural state, able to handle the majesty of this tremendous creature, a symbol of my own inner nature.

A dream which followed some time later told how this untrained power could be dangerous to myself and others.

Darlene Montgomery

85

A young woman enters a shopping mall where many are walking and shopping. She moves casually through the mall followed by her pet leopard. The cat starts to attack several people who are walking in the complex. As myself and others hide up on a higher level we urge her to take control of the animal.

I spent some time with the dream trying traditional ways of unlocking its meaning. Then I allowed myself to become the cat, (a technique for dream awareness) and realized what it was telling me.

The woman was myself innocently strolling through life with her strong and uncontrollable instincts. In the early years of my own spiritual search for truth, I felt it was my duty to instruct others using my instincts and dreams.

An underlying arrogance dismissed me from seeing their ability to follow truth in their own way. Not realizing the power of my opinions, I would unintentionally maul others emotionally, mentally or spiritually.

I still had not learned the law of silence which dictates that truth passed to us through the inner channels is for our own awareness and not to be imposed on others.

Now at this important juncture I had to come to terms with this subtle aspect of discrimination. Misuse of power is the clear lesson here.

Many years earlier, I was living with a man whom I loved very much. I spent a good deal of the time telling him how I knew this, or how my dreams said that. I selfishly expected him to glean the same perceptions from my inner guidance without giving him an opportunity to arrive at his own answers. It was simply a form of naive spiritual arrogance on my part.

Once, when I was being more preachy than usual, my three-and-a-half-year-old daughter Jessica piped up with, "Truth is just for us, isn't it Mommy?" At first my ears screened out her words as they were disguised amongst her typically childlike babbling. Then I grasped the simple wisdom.

Spirit had used her to relay an important message; information which is given via the inner channels was for my own use.

This lesson of discrimination was only beginning to make itself known to me.

Mama exhorted her children at every opportunity to "jump at de sun." We might not land on the sun, but at least we would get off the ground.

~ Zora Neale Hurston

—————— Finding a Voice

In an attempt to find wholeness, I had spent the last ten years studying the nature of opposites.

At first, I had cherished the feminine as the way to truth while almost completely ignoring the fact that wholeness requires balance. Now I had come to realize that there was more to the art of balance than clinging to one side of life.

My fear of success and money had deep roots in many of my past lives. After spending so much time favouring the passive side of life, the qualities of the masculine side of my personality lay dormant.

This dream showed my progress in developing the correct relationship toward this male self.

I am attempting to carry a very heavy baby boy up a flight of stairs. At the bottom I had left my purse and valuables. Someone at the bottom would bring my purse once I reached the top.

Dream Yourself Awake

This dream showed that there would be a number of steps to the process of healing and integrating the male qualities I was introduced to. There was to be an uphill climb but in the end I would earn the right to my own self-sufficiency (purse).

In my relationships I was constantly searching for a deeper meaning to the events around me. Unwilling to accept rational explanations for the synchronistic occurrences around me, I became the hound of heaven. I wanted something more and was willing to expose the truth whenever necessary.

I began to discover that my brash method of pointing out truth was disturbing to some. Now I was on my own and facing truth became a very subjective experience. I reviewed my attitude in a series of dreams which mirrored back my fear.

In one such dream I was dating a man. I had to keep our relationship secret because he didn't want others to know. For some reason the answer seemed to be that I must date his father. I kept up the facade until I could stand it no longer. I finally told my love that I couldn't live that way any longer. He would have to tell the truth or I would leave.

This dream shows one of the other roles of the parasite which is protection. By dating those who were cautious of my brand of truth, I had found opportunities to hide my true nature even to myself. I was learning to balance the brash way I imparted truth. By living amongst those who feared the kind of spiritual intensity I often displayed, I had found the perfect place to conceal my real power.

As far back as grade six the lesson of hiding my voice had appeared. My search for connection and communication could only come about when I learned to trust once again in my ability to discriminate in matters of speech.

Another dream showed me the trust that was developing with my male nature.

There is a long haired man. He knows we are going to be together and he tells my ex-boyfriend Sean. His certainty frightens me and I'm afraid he will reveal to Sean some of the spiritual truths which allowed him to arrive at his conclusions. Fortunately, my new man is very insightful and is able to let Sean know without revealing his sources.

In order to mend the fracture of trust in the bridge between truth and silence, I suffered through a number of relationships where communication was a real effort.

This truth was given to me to learn to find a voice again in awkward conditions. I was introduced to those who had fears about spiritual truth to teach me the art of discrimination. It wasn't so much what I said but that I could find a way to speak with ease and confidence again.

There is a time for the law of silence and a time for the law of honesty. In many cases it was more important for me to speak up since this was where my greatest fears lay.

Where the law of silence and honesty meet is the fine line of discrimination. Giving truth to those who hadn't earned it had created the karmic pattern now playing out in my life..

This dream of healing brought to light an awareness of the growth which had indeed taken place whereby a trust had formed between my inner self and the spiritual source of good.

The walls of my self-created prison were slowly melting away, making the world a safer place to express myself.

The old question, "Why are men afraid of powerful

women?" posed to me by the taxi driver some twenty or so years before was finally being answered.

Come out of the circle of time
And into the circle of love.

~ Jalaludin Rumi

———— Beyond the Dream

At times we are moved to change something in our patterns of behaviour, work or relationships. This instinctive urge drives us on in spite of the discomfort we know our change will inevitably cause.

These silent nudges are the clarion call of Soul as it urges us from a resting place on our journey home to God.

Soul's goal and only goal is to travel back home to God and to become a co-worker. The Law of Growth spurs us on to our greatest goal of spiritual freedom.

The call of Soul asks that we respond with inspired leaps of faith into unknown territories of our inner landscapes. For many who believe in fate, there is an unknown and ominous future awaiting around each corner. But Soul is a creative entity that brings dreams into reality by way of our creative imagination and not some outside cause.

The call of Soul came to me one day. At the time I was in a good relationship. We both were happy. Then a distant vibration, an echo in time, began to shake my spiritual foundation. At first

  Dream Yourself Awake

it came like a faint breeze that signals the change of weather. Then the call grew louder and settled in like the first frost of autumn.

I felt a tug at my innermost being telling me to move on. Two months later I was still trying to ignore the impulse while a terrible discomfort grew inside me.

Then one evening I went to the movies with a group of friends. The film, called *Always* starred Richard Dreyfuss as Pete, a daredevil pilot who's passion is fighting forest fires. Pete enjoys the thrill of living life on the edge. It isn't uncommon for him to fly until his fuel gage reads almost empty. Once in a while he even runs out of fuel and has to glide his heavy metal plane above the treacherous tree tops to make an emergency landing.

Dorinda, Pete's girlfriend, is a radio dispatcher and often waits breathlessly each time for Pete to narrowly avoid his demise.

Dorinda, exasperated by the numerous time she's witnessed his stunts, gives him an ultimatum, either Pete hangs up his wings and takes the job offer as Commander at a training school in Flatrock Colorado, or their relationship is over. Pete jokes with Dorinda about how her life would be without him and says, "You're never going to be with another man because you're never going to get over me."

The next morning as he boards a small plane in preparation for the first flight of the day, Dorinda hops on her bike and rides furiously over to where Pete is in the pilot's seat. Climbing up the ladder to the cockpit, she tells Pete, "I don't want you leaving the ground without telling you I love you."

Again they banter back and forth as Dorinda tries to get Pete to use the words he's never been able to say. As Dorinda walks away Pete calls after her, "I love you," but the engine roar drowns out his words.

Darlene Montgomery

He takes off and once more flies into the furnace-like flames. Pete's best friend Al experiences a fire in one engine when his plane catches the flaming tree tops. Pete uses ingenuity by flying over Al and releasing the load of red watery mud intended for the flaming forest below.

But now Pete's plane is caught in a dive and while struggling to pull up he hits the tree tops and his own engine catches fire. In a sudden blast his plane explodes in a ball of fire.

A moment later Pete awakens in a burned out forest. He is met by an angel name Hap on a grassy island. She fills Pete in on his recent demise then gives him an assignment back on earth. Pete is to serve others by giving back some of what he has learned.

Hap says, "Pete, you've had your life. Now anything you do for yourself is a waste of Spirit." Pete is assigned to help another pilot with inspiration and wisdom.

This isn't easy when he realizes his job is to guide Dorinda's new love interest, Ted Baker, in the art of flying. He's in training at The Attack Training Base where Al is now the Commander.

Pete finds his ability to imprint on other people's thoughts amusing and discovers an assortment of ways to play havoc with their lives even guiding Ted to dump a load of thick red mud on Al during a practice run.

When Pete tries to keep Dorinda's affections fixed on him, Hap calls him back to remind him that, "Anything you do for yourself is a waste of Spirit." She continues, "I sent you back to say goodbye and until you do, Dorinda won't be free and neither will you."

And so Pete is wisening to the lesson he must learn.

In the final scene, Pete says to Dorinda, "I could never tell you the way I felt but I'm telling you now, I love you." Pete sees that his lesson was about freedom and says, "To gain your freedom you have to give it. The love we hold back is the only pain that follows us here."

With the lesson learned, Pete says, "I'm releasing you. I'm moving out of you heart. Go to your new life."

When leaving the movie I found myself in a state of shock. My face was a shade of pale white and I walked as if in a trance. Friends showed great concern but I could offer no explantation for this strange and eerie reaction the movie had inspired.

After returning home I found a note on the kitchen counter saying, "Meet me in the theatre to see *Always*". While I watched the movie in one theatre, my partner had gone to some other theatre to see it at the same time.

The whisper that had gnawed at me for several months was now a clanging bell. Each of us had a lesson to learn. I felt like Pete, forced to find out about the deeper lessons of truth.

I knew that my job was to let go and let my partner have another experience. Like the pilot in the film I wasn't to try to alter events.

And so that evening I told my partner I would have to go. He seemed to understand that this was necessary but letting go wasn't easy for either of us.

Learning about freedom was just beginning.

My next relationship had a similar theme as my partner had his own compelling need to move on. Once again I was forced let go of someone I loved.

And the next relationship had the same theme with the same whisper haunting me to move on. Many years later I began to draw a correlation between the film *Always* and the deep lesson of freedom. This spiritual theme was the root lesson of this life. I had come here to learn to grant freedom to others in

Darlene Montgomery

the most trying of circumstances.

As I learned the difficult lesson of letting go, a deep loneliness began to heal. This loneliness was an inexplicable hollowness, a feeling of total and unending isolation that had been there all my life.

Sometimes our changes begin with simple knowing.

Knowing is often harder to master than dreaming, for with knowing there is an absence of explanation. Knowing requires a leap of faith, for the test which accompanies the gift of knowing is total trust in spirit.

The purpose of that leap may remain unclear for quite some time and this is where the mind argues a great deal. At these times dreams are important, for they can provide needed information to knit together the space between what you knew to be true and the time it takes to fully manifest physically.

As time went by I began to see the reasons why change was necessary. I came to understand that after every leap of faith there was an inevitable void.

A void is a place where the rules seem to change and many of the spiritual tools we have used up until then no longer apply. In time the space will be filled with gifts but not necessarily of the type one would expect.

It took many cycles of this nature for me to recognize how Spirit was working with me. At times I would be filled with terror as I struggled to hold onto what I knew to be true. I came to see that each time I let go of something I no longer needed, I was rewarded with fresh insights and greater strength for the journey ahead.

You must have control of the authorship of your own destiny. The pen that writes your life story must be held in your own hand.

~ Irene C. Kassorla

Taking Ownership

After my dream of the white BMW, an inner door began to open for me whereby I was shown another life much different from the one I had been living. In it I could wake up each day knowing that abundance was a natural part of everything. The work was just beginning in the transformation which was necessary in order for that dream to become a reality.

Many times our dreams simply point out the possibilities which can only be brought into reality through our own efforts.

What the dream was offering me had little to do with money and everything to do with spiritual wealth. It was a richness of drinking in God's love, an absolute certainty of my divinity and a childlike wonder for the possibilities awaiting me.

For several weeks I walked in this world, springing with life in every step. Before this could become an absolute reality I would endure a deep inner cleansing. I would have to face the causes which had brought about much of the difficulties in life.

One weekend I attended a course which would give me certification as an Educational Kinesiology™ practitioner.

On the third day of the course I was feeling frustrated as I struggled to break free of the old consciousness. I was still hounded by many of the symptoms of the Eastern Parasite and this week end they all came to the surface. I spent some time lying on the floor completely overwhelmed with self-doubt and exhaustion.

I left early, overcome with frustration at the difficulty I was having in manifesting the state of consciousness I had been promised.

That night as I prepared for sleep, I asked for a dream which might grant me understanding.

I asked, "What is preventing me from having the new vehicle in my life?"

I dreamt I had a brand new car. There were two oriental men sitting on either side of me in the front seat. They tell me I can't afford the car and would have to give it back.

The next morning, the instructor began with a story which drew a parallel to last night's dream. She had worked with an oriental woman who was wealthy and successful, yet had extreme feelings of low self-worth.

The instructor explained that the woman suffered from a miasm (set of emotional, mental or physical patterns) stemming from the Chinese culture which resulted in an obstruction of her enjoyment of her wealth.

This synchronistic anecdote provided me with a timely explanation of my dream. The car as my new vehicle represented my new consciousness which was already in my possession. A long held miasm created from lifetimes in eastern cultures had prevented me from feeling worthy of what I already possessed.

Dream Yourself Awake

The two men portrayed the cause of my problem which stemmed from lifetimes in cultures where women were assigned a status of lesser value to men.

Because Soul is born of a place where time has no limitations, we can journey to any place in our past and future to correct our viewpoint and remove the restrictions we or others may have placed on us.

Laying claim to the inherent riches of my own spiritual birthright was next in what was to come in my own learning. It came through a set of experiences where I would need to stand up for who and what I believed by way of values, decisions and virtues.

*Faith is the bird that feels the light
when the dawn is still dark.*

~ Rabindranath Tagore

The Test of Faith

Understanding the creative nature of Spirit is a step towards true realization of our own interconnected relationship with all life. As we develop a trust in Spirit's ability to design and carry out events in our lives, synchronistic experiences become a normal occurrence.

During one week an important lesson was brought to my attention through the repetition of a theme in three different television shows. The shows portrayed three situations, each similar, yet from different perspectives concerning exploitation in the media.

In two of the shows, the press exploits individuals through erroneous or slanted stories. Subsequently, lives are damaged by the slander. In one film a man loses his job and almost his family due to a university tabloid's inaccurate portrayal of his character.

I wondered at the purpose of this recurring theme. How did this play a part in my own circumstances? Lately I had experienced a deep mood of apathy about my dreams and writing.

It took the repetition of the same theme in very close

Dream Yourself Awake

sequence for me to notice the message.

As I watched the destructive force of the media when given license to falsify stories about others, I viewed some of the history of my past lives. It came to me that some of my apprehension over revealing myself through writing was due to a time where I had failed in my responsibility to maintain the element of truth and discrimination in writing about others.

This is one of the ways dreams filter truth so that we may be protected from the shock that sudden knowledge of our misdeeds might cause.

In the film, *Cry In the Dark* with Meryl Streep, a Christian couple in Australia are charged with the murder of their baby daughter. The media feeds bizarre and fabricated stories to the public who prey on the couple. As the viewer we know that they are innocent.

From the beginning they have a strong trust in God, so strong in fact that the public suspects them of wrongdoing for they appear too detached.

As the story continues, they are put through two rounds of trials. The wife keeps much of her dignity and shows incredible strength and faith, while the husband begins to crumble as the outlook becomes more and more bleak.

At the second trial she is convicted of murder and sent to prison for life. Five years later, the police locate a piece of the child's clothing at a dingo feeding ground, proving the woman's innocence.

This true story was similar to the trials endured by many of the saints and masters throughout history as they strove toward God-realization. Pythagoras, saint and teacher, discovered mathematical theories which changed the face of science. He was hunted down, his school destroyed and many followers killed because his presence threatened the stability of the ruling power of his time.

When we choose to believe that God has forsaken us, we lose the strength and feeling of being supported in our lives.

A dream, which followed shortly after I viewed the film, shed light on my own test of faith.

In the dream a man stands on a tower where his job is to shoot missiles down below. He points to his car which is far below, parked in front of a mansion. His white car is difficult to discern as it stands in front of the white concrete steps of the mansion. There is a row of similar mansions all with white cars in front making it even more confusing for me to tell which is his.

He asks me to feed his dog, a white standard-bred poodle which is inside his mansion. After arriving, I am met by a couple who live in the mansion. Their job is undefined. I look through the cupboards for the right food for the dog. I find a small bowl seemingly for a cat and cat food. I am not satisfied with the amount of food and so after searching for more, find kibble, a hard dry food for dogs. I am relieved knowing this will be substantial.

There are a number of important messages in this dream.

The man high on the pedestal shows a separation has existed between my actions and their effect on the world. The male is untouched by what he is doing to others below. As I jot down the dream, I spell job, "jobe", which prompts me to see the similarity in my recent experiences to the test of faith Job underwent.

The weapons of destruction alluded to the ways I had used

 Dream Yourself Awake

my pen for destructive purposes, a theme already brought to my attention through the previous shows about the press.

Three features in the dream are in white. In the foreground is the vehicle of Soul in white. In the background the mansion is also white. Within the mansion, the white purebred dog. Each are aspects of Soul's refinement.

As we refine our spiritual viewpoint, Soul develops the qualities of seeing, knowing and being. These are the natural attributes that Soul acquires as it travels higher toward its true home.

A white poodle had appeared in many dreams over a period of years but now it was a standard bred poodle and an evolution of this character.

The white standard bred poodle is a link to the earlier dream of the white standard BMW. Both the car and the dog are of a refined quality. Each requires the right fuel to operate. An inner standard had to be met before I could take ownership of that spiritualized consciousness. I needed to find my deeper and substantial instincts equated with my true nature so that I could express myself in the world successfully.

To gain access to new dimensions, I had to solve the riddle of the laws surrounding operating my new vehicle. No substitutes were allowed as indicated with the cat food which symbolized emotions.

The couple portrayed the marriage of Soul, the union of the two and a resolving of polarities. Their neutral relationship was a clue to how to enter the new domain.

These connected waking-and-sleeping dreams, drew a relationship between the factors dividing both past and future and gave a clue as to how I could fuel my new state of spiritual freedom.

Darlene Montgomery 103

I know God will not give me anything I can't handle.
I just wish that He didn't trust me so much.

~ Mother Teresa

———— Beyond the Mind

My days were devoted to writing, public seminars on dreams and other spiritual subjects and music classes which I still taught. I also devoted a certain amount of time to attending to my own recovery through seeing various healers who were able to work with the illusive energy that had caused such debilitating symptoms.

One mustn't be passive, waiting for God to send a miracle. More often we create our own miracles by taking action in our lives. Day after day I experimented with spiritual exercises to find creative ways of resolving the internal conflicts.

In one exercise, I dialogued with the part which I felt was inside me. Day after day I had tried to make contact with this part and to free myself from the still-lingering symptoms.

Finally I stumbled upon a much simpler idea.

After spending many years attempting to come to terms with the roles within my inner universes, I simply decided to focus on the oneness of myself. I brought together all the forces which had before been beside, above or around me, and focused on the one force which was me.

I discovered many things about the mind through this exercise. The mind loves complexity, separateness, struggle and duality and so needs to preserve these qualities in order to maintain authority over Soul.

As long as it is nourished with problems, questions and emotional difficulty, the mind will be in charge of its domain.

As I focused on the oneness of myself and the oneness of Spirit which was myself, the feeling of separateness began to subside. I saw that trying to understand created a perception of duality.

Another side of separateness which the mind enjoys is labels.

One evening, when attending a party at a friend's home, I struck up a conversation with a woman named Joanne. When I told Joanne about my work with dreams she was intrigued. Joanne had recently completed her Ph.D. and was experiencing real difficulty with the transition into the world of public acclaim. She had spiralled into a deep depression and what she described as a black-hole sensation.

Joanne's husband was proud and overjoyed by her achievements and often introduced her with a mention of it. Responses ran along the lines of, "Where did you get your Ph.D?" The mention of a renowned university brought a greater reaction. To be thrust into a position of instant recognition and acclaim was unsettling and caused Joanne to withdraw deep inside herself.

During the course of our discussion we were both shown how our recent accomplishments had created a sort of void. There was a death involved in the achievement of both of our goals.

In my own life I had been giving a series of seminars on dreams and with that came public appearances. With the appearances came public recognition and a feeling of discomfort much like the one Joanne described.

Whenever we achieve a goal which has taken a great deal of time and effort to accomplish, there is often a let down afterwards. Our expectation rarely matches the human experience for when the goal exists to satisfy the ego we are sure to be let down.

Those around Joanne nurtured a false image of how she should feel after attaining her prestigious title. In actuality we don't always gain spiritually through such awards and this can result in feelings of loss. We begin to feel separate from those who look at us in a new way.

After the party, I was left with a feeling of peace and resolution. This meeting marked a turning point as I left behind the illusion I had carried for so long of the social pressure to struggle for recognition. It became evident that degrees and public acclaim could bring a sorrow to the human spirit when there was no spiritual ideal associated with gaining them.

It isn't uncommon to experience a state of incongruity after a significant life achievement. After the birth of my daughter, I felt profoundly ordinary as I looked about at the three other women who occupied my hospital room. These women with oversized breasts and hemorrhoids somehow created a paradox which sent me plummeting into a chasm of disillusion.

I had imagined motherhood to be a noble experience where my body effortlessly yielded forth a seven pound human form.

In the movie, *Local Hero*, a town of Irish peasants are each offered a million dollars for their share of an oil field which occupies their land.

A celebration follows the signing of the final papers but the mood is less than cheerful. One of the town-folk turns to another and says, "This isn't how I thought I was going to feel after receiving a million dollars." In response the other says, "How did you think you were going to feel?"

As I looked for a way to match my inner dreams with my outer goals a dream showed me how our desires can result in disappointment and confusion.

I am in a mansion where a wedding is taking place. After watching the wedding procession, I go to a table where an elaborate display of food is laid out. I make a selection of a piece of cake but am surprised it does not taste sweet. In another room Oprah Winfrey is playing an ancient melody on a four-stringed instrument.

The union of self which I was seeking, and in fact I had already experienced, brought with it the natural abundance of spiritual food. I had expected the marriage or inner union, to provide a sweetness but found instead a discomfort and confusion by the resulting incongruities in my life.

This inner marriage was not the final achievement. Soul in Its ongoing and timeless journey will always be unfolding. Instead we learn to have a relationship with Spirit, the true and eternal aspect of ourselves.

*I am convinced that a woman cannot find her
feminine soul image at all unless she first becomes
on very good terms with her animus. It is he who,
bearing aloft his torch, leads the way into the
innermost recess where the soul image of
a woman so successfully hides.*

~ Irene Claremont de Castillejo (Knowing Woman)

Making Peace With the Pieces

The relationship between men, money and the Eastern Parasite was a tightly knit network of energy that had to be untangled much like a garden hose. It wasn't always apparent where the beginning or the ending was for Soul doesn't view time, and its relationship to events, in a linear fashion.

Within the one giant knot there was also a conglomeration of many smaller knots.

Dreams played a large role in disentangling the knot by giving an overview from one life to the next and back again. As each curtain was pulled back for me to view through the eyes of Soul, there developed a congruency between relationships both inner and outer; past and future; visible and invisible.

Through daily spiritual exercises a transparency grew between the inner and outer worlds.

In this dream that transparency began to reveal the parasite's true nature and purpose in my life.

Two women are in a relationship of a nature which is unclear. One is Japanese. The other Anglo-Saxon. The Japanese woman is returning to her father, a rich oil magnate. She must go and make peace with her father who long ago left the family. The other woman will stay and use the time to sort out details with her family.

In my journal I wrote:

It seems that there were two feminine identities in myself that have formed the basis for my struggle. The Japanese woman is a displaced aspect of my many past lives in eastern cultures, also known as the Eastern Parasite or the sister-self.

She was born out of my rich male energy and moved over to the feminine side of myself causing confusion by bonding so closely as to be undetectable. The Anglo-Saxon sister represents myself in this reality where I have been living with my mother and brother sorting out details of our family history in my present life.

Now as I trace the history of their creation, these parts no longer needed to play the same supportive roles.

The Japanese woman is from within my own rich spiritual energy. As was alluded to in other dreams, the feminine had been preparing to join the masculine to create abundance of Spirit in my life. Her journey back to the rich father is similar to the story of the prodigal son, who returns to the wealth of his true home.

The dreams suggests that I had abandoned my male nature somewhere in my past lives and had been leaning on a pseudo-male energy for support.

The misspelled word, 'Peace' as 'Piece' pointed to the solution through wholeness. At this time bringing the pieces together would restore peace to my world after such a long struggle.

The slow and careful process of listening to Spirit and following my inner guidance had determined my readiness to accept the greater gifts of Spirit.

The process of healing came by letting go of ideas and fears embedded in the various levels of my consciousness. At the same time I was assimilating changes which moved through the various levels of my being.

In the next several months the integration of this dream would take place as another lesson followed.

Dream Yourself Awake

Think of yourself as an incandescent power,
illuminated and perhaps forever talked to by God
and his messengers.

~ Brenda Ueland

The Silver Table

After discovering that the energy of the Eastern Parasite had been created to give myself added strength in order to survive, I began to rearrange much of my thinking about life.

Although, for a long time dreams had tried to tell me that something was not as it appeared, I simply had not filled in enough of the puzzle to grant a clear picture of the truth. The parasite was borrowing energy from within me and sending it where necessary in order to create a support system until my true inner structure could be rebuilt.

Much earlier on, a dream had forewarned me of the restructuring that would take place.

I'm in my mother's basement. She points out two support beams leaning against a wall. She tells me that because they were not put into place when the house was built it would take a much longer time to install them.

The house represented the past and my consciousness which had been built incorrectly without the support system that comes with total reliance on Spirit.

My survival was based on false values, however ripping them out all at once would have caused a collapse of my inner support system. I resisted giving the old away too quickly and accepted the inner changes slowly as the new values and perspectives took shape.

At a turning point, this dream describes how my old state of consciousness comes to an end.

I am in a large mansion. The owner has died and the contents of the will are to be distributed amongst several others. There is a list of items which I may choose from. At first I see that there are two apartments but when I ask, am told they are not available to me. Seeing a large silver table, I decide I will take this. I know it will be very heavy but think it must be very valuable.

The executrix of the will tells me that I must take the table by Tuesday or lose it. I live far away so the journey home and back would make it impossible. I decide to get others to help me.

Then I see a friend of mine. He has made a simple wooden table which is painted in colours from the American Indians.

The dream refers to a deep inner change which emphasizes the death of an old consciousness. At this important crossroad I was trying on the clothes of the past and seeing how burdensome it would be to carry these ideas forward on the road to God.

Instead a more practical, industrious and creative approach is being introduced. The table with its ornate silver engravings speaks of some ancient and elaborate structure.

In contemplation, I discovered the table was the mind, valuable and engraved with details of lifetimes of experience but too burdensome to carry any further into the world of God. If I chose the symbol of the mind I would slip out of rhythm with Soul's desire to return home to God.

When I notice the man and his natural approach to life, I am intrigued. Although the table wasn't made of the type of precious materials in the silver table, I found the creative, physical approach and the natural materials appealing.

The dream was directing me to qualities innate within my being that would make my journey easier. The natural materials were qualities characteristic of Soul; creativity, simplicity and economy. These materials were readily available to me now as the dream showed.

If I chose a more cumbersome approach by continuing in the attitude of materialism, my journey would be long, tiresome and for nothing as the dream showed.

With the death of the old consciousness came a need to disburse old values in the form of my will.

"Thy Will Be Done," was the attitude to which the dream alluded. The old structures were now ready to be moved as I chose to let go of my attachment to an old way of being.

*What seems different in yourself; that's the rare
thing you possess. The one thing that gives each of us
his worth, and that's just what we try to suppress.*

~ Andre Gide (from an unknown work)

Getting to Know Myself Again

Learning to use the qualities seen in my dream of "Thy Will Be Done" required a letting go. Having grown accustomed to the complexities of the mind, I was learning to streamline my relationship to truth. Practise makes perfect was true in this case.

I was yielding to the vision of wisdom and industry seen in the dream. To accompany this period of growth and change, several dreams and outer waking dreams linked together the internal recognition of learning and understanding that I was experiencing.

This episode of "Highway to Heaven" drew attention to a deep lesson of trust.

A family is bound together to care for a man who is severely disabled and mute. They have put their own lives on hold indefinitely to care for George who is now approximately thirty years old. An angel appears in their lives. He convinces the mother and brother to bring George to a clinic where he can be assessed for his abilities.

A series of tests show that George can understand and follow direction and that he has the use of two fingers which will allow him to manoeuvre a computerized hand control. Afterwards he is able to move about in an electric wheelchair and to communicate through the use of an electric keyboard which transcribes George's commands into sound.

Up until now, the mother's fears have prevented George from receiving help. Over the years, her fears have supported many illusions about George's capabilities. Her own prejudices about the medical system has kept her from seeking assistance for her son.

George's brother postponed his marriage plans indefinitely because his mother convinces him that George can't survive without his help.

With his new equipment in hand, George decides he wants to be a writer and surprises his brother by commanding him to go and live his life. He won't be needing the constant care he required in the absence of having a way of communicating his needs.

This story helped me recognize the illusion of disability within myself sustained by my own passivity and prejudice against worldly systems. I had let myself be confined to limitations through fear and narrowness of mind. As I learned to have faith in something greater than myself, I was slowly being freed from limitations seen here as a crippling disease. Now I could express my gift of writing and speaking.

The mother represented an attitude of being overly responsible for others' handicaps while at the same time using care for others as a means of control and an excuse to hold myself (the brother) back from love.

The second show demonstrates the way this attitude had prevented me from achieving my real potential.

An accident has left a man with amnesia. He is taken in by a single mother and they begin a relationship. She knows he has amnesia but fails to help him find his family or to recover his memory. In the meantime his wife is searching for him. She telephones hospitals in an attempt to track him down.

The single mother owns a restaurant. The man helps in her kitchen and in the process discovers his culinary talents.

Later on, the man is recognized at a local restaurant. His true name and profession are revealed as the friend hands him a matchbook featuring the name of a restaurant called, "Allan's". At first Allan is afraid to admit that he might be the person on the matchbook. He has grown accustomed to the false life he has been leading.

Finally Allan contacts his wife through the number on the matchbook. She comes to visit but Allan can't remember her or the love that they used to share. The single mother is frightened that Allan might remember who he is and leave her as she discourages Allan from pursuing any more leads.

Allan's wife leaves behind a folder containing pictures of his family and life before the accident. At first Allan is hesitant to look but eventually he does. While viewing the pictures a flood of memories and feelings rush in. He loves his wife and his family very much. It is where he belongs.

This illustrates the false relationship I had maintained with yet another aspect of the sister-self and the Eastern Parasite. The relationship was based on grounds of selfishness and fear. It was a compensatory situation, meant only for survival in the physical universe.

The true relationship which Soul has with Spirit is conveyed in the forgotten marriage. The divine love contained within the natural union of self-realization can be attained only through a willingness to look at the truth in the form of pictures or in my case dreams.

Returning home to God was the true goal and desire of Soul. The sister-self in the form of the woman who fought to keep the truth from Allan, represents the mind and false self.

Eventually Soul gets tired of living a lie and begins to search for the truth and its true home. Recovering our true identity as Soul means letting go of many of the false identities we have amassed on the long journey of many seasons.

Any goal which keeps us from standing fully in the light of truth and divine love isn't worthy of our efforts no matter how easy or comfortable it may seem.

*Hold fast your dreams! Within your heart keep one
still, secret spot where dreams may go, and, sheltered
so, may thrive and grow where doubt and fear are
not. O keep a place apart, within your heart for little
dreams to go!*

~ Louise Driscoll

Death of an Ideal

One hot summer day, I took a walk with a dear friend called Jane. Our friendship was based on a common desire for truth and most importantly divine love.

While walking and browsing in shop windows, we came upon a book store.

Even now, I rarely felt compelled to read a book from cover to cover, a leftover symptom from my earlier dream of a circle of geese. This time however, my eyes locked onto a small book titled, *Lessons of Love*, by Melody Beattie.

I purchased the book and took it home. The story described a transformation in Melody's life that was brought about by intense suffering. For many years prior to the set of circumstances which led her to write this book, Melody had been a best selling author and public speaker.

After the death of her son in a skiing accident, Melody lost her passion for living. For years, she teetered on the edge of life, caught in intense grief, then depression and eventually apathy.

Over time, she endured a process of healing that opened

Dream Yourself Awake

within her a greater depth of spiritual connection.

One day she inwardly hears the words, "Your message has changed."

Until now, Melody's books had resembled a New-Age psychology with a message that fit the needs of society. Self-management and emotional responsibility were the driving themes.

Melody recognized that the journey of her loss had transformed her relationship to truth and her future writings were to reflect this.

For the past year, my work had been mostly on hold as I turned a corner in understanding my own place in the world as a writer and speaker. I was beginning to see that dreams were only a starting point for understanding mission, but not my mission in itself.

As a way to bring me around to this mission, I landed a position with a large publishing firm whose sole mission was to inspire and uplift through compiling books containing heart-appealing stories. My roll was to collect, read and mark each story by grading it on a scale from one to ten based on each story's ability to uplift the reader.

During this process I began to foster the habit of listening to the rythyms and patterns within the writing which invoke harmonious responses. Just as a mother knows the cry and nuances of her baby's calls, I came to know the shape of these rythyms and to understand the importance of leaving the reader with a way to take a step spiritually through the story's message.

Love is the message but, as in parenting, love comes through in many forms whether through discipline, kindness, firmness, support and at time, silence.

Although there were many times I felt that the universe had

made a grave error in placing me in this position, I came to see and understand that there are never errors in the placement of each Soul's lessons.

Just as a good story has a beginning, middle and end, our journey has its natural order and relationship within the structure of the universe.

I was learning that love was the medium as well as the message from which my own mission would spring forth.

My life has been a tapestry of rich and royal hue,
an everlasting vision of the everchanging view.

~ Carole King

On the Field of Dreams

My journey had led around corners and over miles within my own universes. I had undergone a transformation over the years since the circle of geese. It was much like being born out of a multi-layered cocoon, a slow journey of peeling back layers to reveal the beautiful, soulful expression that was me.

Over time, my outer life was being harmonized with this inner transformation. One by one inner doors led to outer freedom, abundance and creativity.

Now I could see that in spite of everything which had happened to me and all of the apparent difficulties, love was the great healer, the salve in my wounds and the prime mover in all my creative endeavours.

This dream showed me I had arrived at an important crossroads in my journey.

I am staying with a couple temporarily. The wife has bought me home several items as a gesture of appreciation. I hear her husband in another room commenting to his wife about me. He is

angry that I am getting these gifts and I know the wife will be unable to defend me. I gather my things to leave, calling my daughter who is staying there as well. We leave the house and drive away, my daughter in another car. She has difficulty keeping up.

We round a corner and as we near an intersection, I see Kevin Costner standing there. We have worked together before and he leans forward as if there is no windshield on my car and we embrace. Our feelings are tender and natural. How familiar he is to me.

I awoke with the recognition I had made good choices in matters of relationships. The love from within the dream stayed with me most of that day.

The couple were a reflection of relationships of envy, jealousy and anger, a theme that had been at the forefront of my life until now. As I left behind those relationships and people who presented obstacles to my path, my ability to receive the gifts of Spirit increased. Recognizing the importance of moving out of harm's way had earned me the right to move on to new experiences.

The dream was showing me the true nature of this couple and their real attitude toward me. In spite of my friendship with the dream woman and anything she might have given me, I could not postpone my own journey even if she were to hold herself back.

Kevin Costner had held a place in my heart as a symbol of my own search for truth since viewing the film, *Field of Dreams*, several years before. Now, as I was moving towards my own dreams, he represented a mirror of my own future success.

Meeting Kevin, a representation of the inner master or

spiritual guide was my reward for leaving behind an old state of consciousness.

This inner meeting marked a fulfillment of an inner marriage and the promise of my outer dreams coming to fruition.

After all, I was the person in my dreams. The figures and scenes in my dreams were about me and my life; so Kevin Costner was both the outer potential for my creativity to express itself in the world and the promise of love as a harbinger of truth and love.

The future belongs to those who believe
in the beauty of their Dreams.

~ Eleanor Roosevelt

_____ Under the Christmas Tree

As I rounded the corner of this journey, I could see before me the offer of a life which had been promised long ago in the dream of the BMW.

I was to enter a long and intense period where learning the importance of receiving became the backdrop of all life experiences. Something within was beckoning me to open my vision and my heart to a promise of spiritual wealth beyond all of my perceptions, hopes and seeming capabilities.

This test of receiving began to show up both inwardly and outwardly as portrayed in the following dream.

Fred K. has a ruby, bear-paw broach which he wants to give me. I'm not certain that I really want it for something about it makes me slightly uncomfortable. It is so rich and red and full of an ancient wisdom that I wonder at the responsibility of it. Then I remember an agreement I made before this life to accept it when it was offered to me, so I do.

The ruby bear-paw broach was an invitation to embrace the possibilities which were being presented in my life. As the dream indicates, I had made an agreement as Soul prior to this life to meet the challenge of accepting the greater gifts of life.

Learning this lesson was rather long and painful. I had the habit of throwing away gifts because I would often misunderstand Spirit's way of teaching. So often there is a period of discomfort in even the most glorious of circumstances as the consciousness adjusts to new forms of truth.

For a long while, I had seen life through a mist or haze, expecting the worst. It had become a habit which restricted a deeper level of appreciation and gratitude, important factors on the road to God.

This dream reflects an inner change in my own perspectives towards success and abundance.

Jim Carrey is living in my basement. There is a pile of rubbish at the top of the stairs which he has left there. I am dismayed at how much there appears to be and how it blocks the entrance to the basement. A friend, Shelley, appears and lifts the corner of something from the pile. As she lifts it the whole pile shapes itself into an A-line, tent-like Christmas tree.

Jim Carey was a person who had held his dreams close to his heart for many years, by carrying a ten million dollar cheque which he had written to himself, as a reminder of the day when his own goals of landing a major film role would occur.

I too, had carried my dreams close to my heart and as I gained a sense of impending success, those obstacles which had blocked my path were dissolving.

In the dream my friend Shelley appears. Shelley had become a dear and cherished compatriot of the common language of living your dreams. She is also a person who through her very presence clears away a cluttered attitude. Shelly had entered my life as a teacher to help me in cleaning up an attitude of distrust about my own worth.

As she lifted an object from the pile of what to me appeared to be a mess, I saw what was actually a streamlined instrument of gift giving, the Christmas Tree. By clearing away a distorted viewpoint, I was able to gain access to my own success and with it the abundance.

I found many times that when I could manage to become childlike and awestruck, that all sorts of wonderful things would begin to happen. Christmas for me was a time of wonder and certainty that gifts were waiting for me.

The mind was throwing up many barriers to me rounding the corner, but in spite of it all, my dreams were full of images of promise and hope.

Another example of learning to accept the greater role that I was moving into, came through this dream with Oprah.

Oprah invites me to one of her special dinners. I sit around a table with several others as a waiter offers us ices as an appetizer.

These dinners of Oprah's were well known to me and her viewers. Those who were invited to join her at a table in her home while the world watched were treated to stories and delicious treats.

These were more than dinners, they were spiritual meetings or gatherings of women and men who shared the secret dreams of their hearts with the world.

Once again my dreams were showing me that on some level I was part of a greater plan. My dreams held a promise of a greater life filled with opportunities.

The best and most beautiful things in the world
cannot be seen or even touched.
They must be felt with the heart.

~ Helen Adams Keller

The Law of Harmony

One particular theme influenced my life for a period of time and that was the importance of forgiveness.

I would be driving and a song would be on the radio about forgiveness. Every time I looked for the answer to the difficulties in my life it included forgiveness.

In her book, *The Anatomy of Spirit*, Carol Myss refers to the need in many cases for her patients to call their Spirit back to them. In some cases there were old hurts and memories of past traumas that were causing illness and in many cases an inability to move forward in their lives.

When we let our energy pour itself away into the past by hanging on to grudges and hurts we are losing valuable energy.

During this period in my life a friend in a dream said, "Leave the past in the past." How simple and good advice that was.

It is impossible to receive the gifts of Spirit when we hold thoughts of revenge and resentment against others. Learning to forgive myself and others was one of the foremost lessons of my heart and would present itself many times in subtle ways.

Dream Yourself Awake

This dream came as the messenger of this news.

I am driving when I suddenly remember a class I am to teach at two o'clock at a school across town. Looking at my watch, I realize I have only five minutes to get there and am certain I can't make it in time.

Suddenly I am there in the school and am looking for a place to stash a heavy grey carry-all. I go upstairs to the classroom. The teacher begins to tell me that the janitor and others don't like the way I have left many of the desks in a mess by using blood and other substances during my classes.

Looking at her desk, I notice that it is stained with markers and other things and wonder why she would complain about me when she obviously was making a mess herself.

After we argue for a few minutes, I decide it is time to teach. I stand up and tell the children to gather round, but none of them move. Again, I instruct them to come around but none of them get up. The teacher then tells me it is four o'clock and school is over.

I am distressed because I realize I won't get paid. The teacher enters the room and leans toward me. At first I am holding a grudge and turn my head away. Then I realize I may not have this opportunity again and I say I'm sorry. Instantly my heart fills with love and I lean over and kiss her cheek. She hands me a cheque. In that instant I recognize her as someone from my physical life I have come to regard as a spiritual mentor.

I had been a teacher of music over the last ten years and the school environment was familiar. Recently my classes were coming to a completion as I was rounding the corner to new opportunities.

In my work, I had used a baggage carrier to lift my assorted equipment up stairs and over distances where it would have been awkward and tiring. Now the carrier seemed to be a symbol for the things I had been carrying in my consciousness which needed to be let go.

The time factor between two and four o'clock spoke of the levels of consciousness known as the Astral and the Mental plane, located at the second and fourth plane of Spiritual Space.

By indicating that school was over, my inner guide using the form of a teacher, was telling me that I needed to complete the lessons of this cycle. The underlying test in the dream was in whether I would hold on to my resentments.

The friction between the teacher and myself was the dream master's way of reflecting the particular attitude which had been the source all my difficulties. Life often sends teachers who reflect our own inadequacies. Those people and situations in my life which had caused me the most grief were to teach me to let go of pride, judgement and selfishness, as the dream conveyed when exaggerating key scenarios.

Spirit was showing me that regardless of anything which may have happened between myself and another, it was all for my education and ultimately my choice to forgive. Without letting go of the past there was no room for the gifts of Spirit as I had been shown for so long through my dreams and contemplations.

In the end, as my heart opened to the teacher, I recognized her to be a dear spiritual friend and co-worker serving in a high capacity within my spiritual community. I was unable to recognize this aspect of myself until the moment I had let go of resentment.

This was an accurate reflection of my life where certain relationships challenged me on this issue.

Do the thing you fear,
and the death of fear is certain.

~ Ralph Waldo Emerson

Worthy

In my work as a speaker about dreams, one key point stands out overall: in most cases dreams are in some way helping individuals to prepare for change.

Dreams of falling elevators, racing cars or homes with windows which can't be opened in some way reflect the relationship between the inner change and the outer life. We may feel out of step, unprepared, afraid or simply ill at ease, prior to a change in our lives.

This dream tells me where I am in relationship to my own changes, and the work that needs to be done to prepare.

I'm at home when someone knocks at the door. I answer to find a young, attractive, blond German man. He asks for something in German or a language I can't understand. After a moment of trying to understand, I ask him to come in and look around. Then I realize the place is empty except for some leftover traces of trash and it looks like I am moving.

Darlene Montgomery

He turns around and leaves. I feel badly for I am attracted to him. Looking out the window, I see his car and observe that a woman is with him. I think to myself, he has a girlfriend already.

Then I see it's actually a small child and I see that she looks like me. He points to me and says to the child, "She looks like you."

The man at the door is a representation of love and wholeness. He comes from Germany, a country once divided by a wall separating east from west. Now as the country struggles to integrate its two halves there is some turmoil.

The language barrier indicates the foreignness I feel towards the part of myself I have been separate from for so long. I had been isolated in myself but now a movement will occur as demonstrated by the empty house.

I feel inadequate because of his beauty and purity. But we are already one, as the dream shows, for the child is the evidence of the consummation of our relationship. The child is the product of our union and she looks like me. This speaks of the "I am" taken from various holy writings indicating Soul seeing itself as pure Spirit and knowing that it is One with Itself.

To claim this for myself the dream pointed to the test of self-worth that was to follow. In the next while my lessons and life experiences would begin to prove this point.

Dream Yourself Awake

Work is love made visible.

~ Kahil Gibran

Dweller On the Threshold

In Paul Twitchell's Book, *The Flute of God*, he discusses the terror that Soul may experience when crossing the threshold of heaven. As he says, "Soul may linger for years in the position of desiring the inner plane, while quaking in terror at what might happen if he turns loose the outer Self."

As years went by on my own journey, I regarded myself as a dweller on the threshold. The fear which sometimes seemed to overwhelm me had no relationship with anything I could pinpoint. I spent long hours deliberating on how to let go or surrender my life to Spirit.

This dream gave me encouragement that I could begin to make my home in the higher world of pure Spirit as I learned to accept the greater gifts of Spirit in my life.

I find myself in Paris. I'm in a store shopping, looking at prices to see if I can afford the merchandise. From what I have heard of Paris, it is extremely expensive, but when I look at the cost of several items, I find that they are comparative to what I

know. I think to myself that if I get a job here I can easily get by.

A young girl comes along and pulls me into a room and asks me to help a lady. I say, "I don't work here". When I look down I see that there is a small object like a paper clip stuck between the floor and edging. The woman easily removes it.

The dream is showing me that many of the doubts I have about my ability to live in this plane known as Paris are based on hearsay and not truth.

As I am dreaming I realize that Paris is another name for the Soul plane which is the home or first dwelling place of Soul and that plane where there are no dualities. The words, "Pair is", is registered and repeated within the dream, to translate the deeper meaning of Paris to be a mending of the pairs or the halves.

Within the dream, a spiritual principle is shown to me through the feeling of what it would be like if I knew I could live here. There were two prominent lessons hidden within the scenarios of the dream: One is in learning the principle, act "as if" ; two, is in recognizing that when we are asked to serve Spirit, it is never beyond our means to do so.

Acting "as if", means adopting the perspective that I already live here and now in the state of consciousness that I am able to encompass. The feeling in the dream was that it would be easy for me to live anywhere if I could only make the transition through assuming that I was supported by Spirit everywhere I go.

To live as Soul we must become selfless in our approach to life. When being asked to help, I took a position that I didn't work here, showing that I had not yet caught up to the inner potential. The paper clip was the connecting link which would

Dream Yourself Awake

draw me across the threshold to this higher state. It represented an almost indefinable quality that had to be incorporated into both my inner and outer life.

Living in the present moment sounds easy enough, however, the mind likes to categorize, frame, list, analyze, refer to and calculate endlessly in order to satisfy itself. Shifting to the present moment requires that we give the mind a job to do first. Often, when sitting in contemplation, the mind would grow restless as I used the faculties of imagination – seeing, knowing and being to explore and reason.

Ignoring the mind was pointless, especially in light of the fact that it seemed to grow more restless in my attempts to calm it.

On one occasion, I gave the mind a list of things to do as I ran through a door at the other end of a large room. My first attempt failed for the mind still wanted more to do. This time, I gave it a car to drive, a mathematical formula to calculate and a few other things to do. This worked and as I ran through the door, I was in the Soul body and at first had no idea how to operate in that state of pure Soul.

Up until now, my mind had kept me so busy, that I had little time to learn how to just be. I was aware of an ability to see, to know and a perspective of stillness, but beyond that I wasn't certain of what to do. Learning to live and operate in the world of pure Spirit was my next step.

*When we quit thinking primarily about ourselves
and our own self-preservation, we undergo a truly
heroic transformation of consciousness.*

~ Joseph Campbell

The Spell is Broken

Spirit always finds creative ways to disclose its greater vision for our lives by designing unique metaphors and circumstances which will draw out our latent talents and skills.

One particular film granted me a humorous example of one of the ways Soul crosses the borders of the mind worlds.

The movie, *Bell, Book and Candle*, starring Jimmy Stewart, Kim Novac and Jack Lemmon was about a coven of witches living in New York City. Jimmie Stewart's character, Shephard Henderson, is a publisher and practical business type. Kim Novak who plays Gillian, pretends to be writing a book about real witchcraft. She uses it to get revenge against another witch, her rival, by casting a spell which will make Shephard Henderson fall in love with her.

In spite of an aversion to human emotion, Gillian becomes the victim of her own spell when she begins to fall in love with Shephard. Eventually Shephard, believing he is in love with her, asks for her hand. Prior to the love spell, he was engaged to another woman.

With the advent of love, Gillian discovers her conscience and decides to tell Shephard the truth about being a witch. She is now considering the idea of marrying him. At first Shephard doesn't believe that magic exists but in time he sees the truth.

In anger, Shephard seeks out Gillian's rival who gladly reverses the spell. When Gillian realizes she has lost control over Shephard, she threatens to cast a spell on his fiance to whom he is threatening to return.

But when Gillian attempts to use her magic, it fails to work and she becomes furious. Unexpectedly, tears begin to flow down her cheeks. She is crying for the first time. Witches don't cry for they don't feel emotions as humans do. Gillian has become human for she has fallen in love and with love her powers of magic are gone.

The next time Shephard appears Gillian is a changed person. For the first time she knows the feeling of losing someone she loves – she is human and much more humble. At seeing Shephard, Gillian begins to cry. He moves to comfort her. At once, they realize their love for each other. Shephard says, "Perhaps it was love all along for after all, what is magic?"

The dividing line between mind and soul is love as the movie expresses in its childlike way. Up until now Gillian used magic as an expression of power in an attempt to gain control of the events in her life. Using power as her main expression had left no room for love to enter. When love enters the picture, an inner division is naturally crossed and one is transported beyond the mind and power, into the pure worlds of Soul.

Finally, what is magic but an attempt to gain for ourselves the thing known as love.

One of my favourite stories called, "The Golden Dream," by Heather Hughes-Calero, describes the trials of Milarepa, a Tibetan saint who gains God-Realization while under the tutelage of his master, Marpa.

In the beginning Milarepa's mother sends him to be educated in the ways of black magic. The mother enlists him to seek revenge for her family when after the death of Milarepa's father, an aunt snatches the family estate out from under them and forces them into slavery.

Later, the master Marpa, selects a way of ridding Milarepa of the effects of black magic by having him build a series of stone houses. At first Milarepa rebels at the extreme conditions he must endure as he constructs house after house made of single stones.

He must replace the stones with completely new ones each time he is told to begin construction of a new house. His hands and feet are cut and raw from handling the sharp stones.

Many times, Milarepa is confused and angry at the seeming ridiculous task his master has assigned him and each time Marpa tells him he may leave if he desires.

Finally, after Milarepa betrays Marpa, he is told to move on. At this point, Milarepa, in complete despair, settles down to building the house without any qualms, conditions or anger. After a year, Milarepa has completed the house and has surrendered any arguments he may have had within himself over his task. At that point Marpa appears.

In the end, Milarepa comes to know that building each new house was the purification of his consciousness. Each stone he laid upon his house must be pure and done for the effort of itself, for in the end he was not building the house for Marpa at all.

    Dream Yourself Awake

In each story, the characters must cross the line between power and love. Living fully in the presence of love means surrendering all attempts to manipulate Spirit or another to our own ends.

When we realize that Spirit wants us to experience ourselves as its offspring and that it loves and desires to protect us, we lose the need to struggle and bend the spiritual power to our will.

I have learned this at least by my experiments:
That if one advances confidently in the direction of
his dreams, and endeavors to live the life which he
has imagined, he will meet with a successs unexpect-
ed in common hours.

~ Henry David Thoreau

My Father's House

In spite of all my fears, whenever I took the time to sit down and focus on spirit and the inner sound of God, the doubts within my mind were inevitably replaced with the presence of love.

I was growing to understand that love in all its simplicity was at times expressed in patience and other times in action. I had grasped many of the lessons which had occupied so much of my energy, yet the lesson of self-worth was a daily affair where I had to claim the land which I had inherited, guarding it from spiritual thieves.

My life had become the field of dreams where at every turn I listened for the plaintive whisper of God's sentinel. As I moved further into my world of writing I was given encouragement through this dream.

A man approaches me. Studying me for a moment, he offers his diagnosis of my spiritual condition, "I can tell you're a scribe by your forth."

The dated language is the dream's natural clue to my own history. A scribe was a translator of wisdom. His job was to record the words of kings, pharaohs and to interpret the laws. A scribe in Egypt was responsible for recording the words of the Pharaoh on the walls of the temple.

When I went to the library to look up the meaning of the word "forth," I found that its use dated back many hundreds of years. The context in which it could be used was so varied that at first I was overwhelmed.

Finally I saw the meaning which seemed to fit: "To have one's forth, to have outlet or free course, as in; Obstacles...which all must be done and voided before the Pope can have his forth."

Now that I took to heart the messenger's words in my dream, a new page of my own history was being written.

As long as thy mind continues within thee in its present state, even the love for the beautiful, it is pouring its God energies into the external world and unbalancing Soul's forces.

~ Rebazar Tarz

Thy Will Be Done

After the dream of the ruby bear-paw broach, my life took a sharp turn into a period of great pain and struggle. The gnawing at my spirit to achieve the spiritual potential I'd been shown was excruciating at times.

Two things seemed to hang in the balance: (1) my ability to accept the gifts life was offering me, (2) letting go of the past while forgiving myself and others.

A great pain still hung over my heart and along with the pain was an inner struggle to surrender my will to Spirit or to resist.

I wanted to surrender more than anything else, however something inside thwarted all my attempts to let go of certain concepts. I ran up against a wall which seemed intent on stopping me from receiving the gift of the ruby bear-paw broach.

One morning I arose as usual at 8:30 a.m. to do my spiritual exercise. I'd awakened with a heavy heart, even though my inner guide had appeared that night in an unusual setting where he told jokes in a casual manner, giving rise to great peals of laughter from myself and others.

As I went into contemplation, my attention was brought back to many years ago when I had this dream experience.

Along the screen of my inner landscape a voice tells me, "You committed suicide."

The day I first realized that I had committed suicide, many questions were answered for me. A lifetime of emotions and difficulties pointed to how I had imposed my will over the will of Spirit.

The agreements we have made prior to entering a lifetime involve a complex network of individuals all meeting for the specific set of lessons agreed upon by the group. Those plans, which have been created for the benefit of others who are to partake in experiences with us, are thwarted when we take our life.

As years went by I was given liberty to see the many occasions I had taken my life. Much like the Scrooge who stole Christmas, I was invited to view my own past to see where I had caused my misfortune. I had pitted my will against the will of Spirit time and again, not trusting myself to have the courage, strength and ability to fulfill my lessons, and not trusting in God to guide me.

Now many years and lifetimes later, as I truly desired to surrender and accept the greater gifts of spirit, I came up against this great wall.

A deep chasm had formed between Spirit and myself where now I had to prove my own ability to trust even in the darkest of times. The height of the wall was simply a reflection of the scar inflicted on myself each time I resisted the will of Spirit.

In a spiritual exercise I began to simply listen to the voice of

Spirit. It took effort to still the rigid control of my own will and submit to the will of Spirit. By simply listening to the sound of God and flowing with Its presence, ever so slowly the inner resistance was melting away.

Dream Yourself Awake

I found I had less and less to say, until finally,
I became silent, and began to listen. I discovered
in the silence, the voice of God.

~ Soren Kierkegaard

Living in the Certainty

As we grow in awareness, our way of relating to life is redefined. Where once we pleaded for answers, there is an acceptance of what is. Where once we looked outwards for truth, now we are becoming truth.

In our new relationship with Spirit, a trust develops between you and It. At a certain point a bridge is crossed.

The key to crossing that bridge lies in the quality of imagination. We are practising the qualities that we want to become. We hold the image of that which we desire to become. When we allow doubt to take over, we slip out of harmony with Spirit.

The world of Spirit and mind are divided by a fine line. There can be a startling contrast in how we relate to life when we forget our relationship to God. Without that connection to our infinite source we lose sight of the gifts of God that are everywhere.We may then try to do something extraordinary to find that relationship again by pushing at the door of Soul.

The following dream tells me that magic is that fine line that can put me right back where I was.

I am in a place like Niagara Falls where I have been exhibiting feats of magic on the Niagara River. I am arrested by a woman who tells me I must pay to get back to shore.

In the meantime, I am to be held in a holding cell which I must enter through an extremely narrow entrance covered in green slime. I manage to get through and am waiting. A whole world exists down there and I am wondering why people would live there. I am assigned a job noting those entering and leaving and how much they are paying to leave.

I awoke astonished and dismayed that I was still learning to avoid the use of magic in my life. Going to the dictionary, I looked up the word magic to see if the definition might spark an understanding of how I was slipping into its use.

> "Magic adj. & n. (Of) the pretended art of influencing events by occult control of nature or spirits, witchcraft; mysterious agency or power.
> ~ Websters 1970"

I looked back over the events of late to see what I might have been doing to influence the outcome in any way. I used a technique where one asks a question, then opens a book (usually one offering spiritual guidance) at random with the intention of finding the answer to a life problem or in this case a dream.

This is what it said:

"The chela (student) must assume the feeling of already being in the state of God awareness. The crucial point is living within the core of the God State, and never hoping that you

    Dream Yourself Awake

might. (*Anitya* by Paul Twitchell.)

In reading this, I was led back to my dream from a week before of being in Paris . In it, I was shown that acting "as if " was the key to freeing myself from magic.

I had gone through a period of extreme doubting and pleading with God. In that way I had slipped out of trust with Spirit.

Magic was simply a lack of working in the fullness of my potential and an indication of being in the human consciousness where the normal day-to-day struggle of survival causes us to try to manipulate the forces of nature.

In the dream, the holding cell represented the worlds of the mind, and the people who lived there were those who had yet to pass through the narrow door.

Learning to live in certainty was the master passkey to moving beyond the worlds of fear, hesitation and manipulation.

Sometimes we turn to God
When our foundations are shaking
Only to find out that it is God
Who is shaking them ...

~ Anonymous

Representing the President

The old habits of control, fear and power, which kept me in the worlds of the human consciousness, continued to arise as I learned to see the subtle ways I had allowed myself to be victim to both outside and inside influences.

First, letting go of self-concern was necessary. The following dream came as a way of leading to a new awareness.

I'm in the home of a friend of mine. There are several others with us. My friend comes over and puts his hand on my breast. I feel guilty but don't want him to stop either. I go to take a shower for we are preparing to go somewhere. Upstairs in the bedroom is a woman. She is extremely elegant and classy. On the bed are several items of beautiful and expensive clothing. She says something about the display, like they represent the president.

Two items in the dream pointed to the paradox of my inner lesson: (1) letting go of guilt for past choices, (2) feeling worthy to assume a role of female leadership.

Lately, as I geared up for a new spiritual cycle, I had faced a great deal of internal cleansing and purification. One of the questions I'd asked myself was, "Am I worthy of representing a higher state of consciousness?"

The person in my dream was a man mentioned in an earlier dream who had gone from poverty to wealth by using spiritual principles. Along the way he also mixed in some other elements of subtle manipulation and created a debt load of karma so that now his life was falling apart.

My attraction to him or failure to say no to him in the dream was Spirit's way of showing me a relationship to patterns of guilt and a distrust of my own choices.

In a spiritual exercise that day, my spiritual eye opened so that I could see the lesson of excessive self-blame. To move to the next level where the finer spiritual consciousness was waiting, I needed to see myself differently.

Rather than being concerned for what I didn't want to be, it was easier and more beneficial to simply move into life with a natural confidence and forget the things of the past. The woman on another level was a spiritual ideal that I had created by the dreams, hopes and constant longing to become her.

The clothes laid out were available at the moment I chose to assume my role as a representative of love and forget the mistakes of my past.

For life is the mirror of King and slave,
'Tis just what we are and do;
Then give the world the best you have,
And the best will come back to you.

~ Madeline Bridges (1844-1920)

When Laws Change

God catches our interest through the heart. The beauty in the eyes of a child and the whispering laughter of autumn leaves is all God in expression.

Often, in our impatience, we wonder at the course our life has taken. Why did God take me down this street, when it is obvious to me the other street is the better way? Our urgency to achieve our goals causes us to lose sight of the simple ways God is guiding us everyday.

Sharpening our ability to hear the whisperings of Spirit is a daily process.

The following childlike film seemed to warn me to get back in step with this childlike attitude.

Catherine is a dentist. Her friend encourages Catherine to get off the fence and participate in life because her life revolves around work and a self-centered approach to living.

Until now Catherine has avoided invitations to be involved in social events and to let others into her life, especially male

Dream Yourself Awake

relationships. She spends a great deal of time alone in her apartment watching videos and eating popcorn.

One afternoon as Catherine and her friend are at lunch, Catherine is hit by a bike which throws her into traffic. A moment later, Catherine finds herself in limbo, the place between heaven and earth.

While in limbo, Catherine is to be assessed on her life and eventually to be placed either back on earth or sent to hell.

Off to one side, we see a sign posted above the Hellivator which is delivering a gentleman to the depths below where he will serve his time in hell.

Catherine's career on earth as a dentist doesn't go over well in limbo and as a result she is assigned to do community service on earth in the role of the tooth fairy. Once she has completed her term, she will be assessed and a determination made whether she will be sent to heaven or hell.

Certain guidelines go with the job, one of them stating that she is not to interfere in the lives of humans.

As Catherine attempts to master the art of flight, her landings are less than graceful. Her first evening at the job, she stumbles into the bedroom of a young boy of around nine or ten. His mother has died recently and his father spends a great deal of time away.

Bobby, as he is called, wakes up to see Catherine standing over his bed. As time goes by Catherine is drawn back to Bobby and a friendship develops. As children do, he continues to lose his baby teeth and lays them on his pillow.

Meanwhile, Bobby tells a friend that he has met the tooth fairy. His friend lets it leak out to other children. Soon, Bobbie's schoolmates are extracting their own teeth in an effort to meet Catherine. Catherine helps each child in some way to improve

Darlene Montgomery

their lives and eventually she comes to love them each in their own way. A special love develops between Bobbie and herself.

Judgement day comes and Catherine is sent before a panel of six judges all named Joe. Catherine is in trouble because of her interference but is given one more week to prove herself.

Back on earth, the parents are very upset by what is going on and want Bobby expelled from school. Catherine decides she must make herself visible to the parents to prove that Bobby is not fabricating the tale. As adults, they are unable to see the tooth fairy as is true of all who have lost their baby teeth.

Catherine is uncertain how to make herself visible, but her teacher from limbo explains that revealing herself is the secret.

Finally Catherine leans over to hug Bobby and with a great outpouring of love she becomes visible. In this way Bobby's innocence is established. At that point, Catherine, having completed her term of service, is led back to limbo by her guard.

She is judged undeserving and sent to the hellivator. As the hellivator descends, the events of Catherine's life are flashed before us. The next moment she awakens back at the same spot where she was first hit by the bike. She has been given another chance to live.

Immediately, Catherine, who recognizes the great gift she has been given, begins to give of herself in ways she wouldn't before. One afternoon Bobby comes for a check-up. He is a new patient and recognizes Catherine. She tells Bobby that it is time for him to lose his last baby tooth. She easily pulls it out and instantly he loses his ability to recall his experiences with the tooth fairy.

His father enters the office and recognizes Catherine for he was among the parents at the moment of her appearance. They look into each other's eyes and there is an attraction.

He turns to leave but Catherine, remembering her lesson, runs after them and asks them to join her at a baseball game that weekend.

And so Catherine begins to love again.

Awakening my own childlike spirit was the message of this story. It was time to come out of my self-induced exile from humanity that I had imposed upon myself some years prior. Most importantly I needed to find that quality again which gave meaning to my life.

That night I had this dream.

A witch is threatening to destroy another woman and me . We devise a plan to use magic against her. The other woman is to count to three as I sweep a broom around the witch. Somehow the woman has forgotten how to count to three. I decide to do it myself. As I count to three the witch turns into a little girl who is apparently her real identity. The little girl exudes a feeling of freedom and love.

Upon awakening, I was reminded of the story of "The Little Witch" from my childhood. Releasing the child from within the witch, was in fact very much like the story of Catherine who lost touch with her own childlike spirit. Somewhere along the way my own childlike spirit had become encased in a suspicious and fearful shell. Just as Catherine had become mean-spirited and jaded from too much of the wrong kind of experience, a child who is constantly exposed to despair and pain becomes hardened to beauty and most of all love.

The woman who couldn't count to three was a reflection of the forgotten approach of simplicity and childlike ease (as easy as one, two, three) that had been so natural to me earlier in my life.

As I went through the changes in my outer life, a great fear swept over me. For four weeks I had been ill with a severe flu and cough which in spite of herbal remedies, antibiotics and vitamins continued to progress. This inner siege represented the last stronghold of the Eastern Parasite within my consciousness.

This dream tells of an inner healing which is occurring.

I am in a huge hotel with an enormous entrance of yellow marble. I know it must be the largest in the world. In a storage room are boxes of kittens sealed in packages. I feel an urgent need to release them from the air-tight containers. I release one group and place them on a blanket.

Another woman is there but she doesn't want me to release the other box. She shoves them in boiling water and I am angry at her. Somehow I end up taking an elevator to the top of a mountain where a path winds out to another entranceway.

At the top is an older woman. She needs help so I take her back onto the elevator which is now a train. I hold on to the old woman for she is afraid. Once we get down a steep incline I begin to sing, "These are a few of my favourite things."

I start feeling happy and another younger woman begins to join in and we do a harmony. She tells me she was recently in a play.

I saw a theme growing between the recent movie of Catherine, the dream of the witch who was a child and this dream. I saw that the dream pointed to where some part of my expression was locked away and how anger played a part.

The kittens were the fragile child-like feelings and qualities

 Dream Yourself Awake

that I had neatly and conveniently packaged and filed away in an effort to survive in a grown-up world. The woman who didn't want me to release them had been in my life and dreams for the past several years. She had been single for as long as I'd known her and was very much like Catherine who had a career but no other life.

The old woman was myself growing old prematurely and overwhelmed by fear of life. Now as Soul I was urging myself to get back into life even though it was scary.

I sat down to sing Hu and do a spiritual exercise. As soon as the word Hu left my lips, I began to experience a presence of love and calm like being in warm water. My heart was tight with fear and bottled up emotions. I spoke to my heart saying that it was safe to feel and safe to experience the childlike feelings within my being. Soon the love began to flow and I started to recall so many years before when I first decided to close off the feelings after a difficult and painful relationship.

But by bottling up my feelings I had closed the door to love. The power of my decision to exile my emotions was represented in the witch who had taken over the child's body.

Now life had brought me back to myself, my feelings were coming back and with them an awareness of the importance of my favourite things. The harmony in the dream with the woman was myself coming back to harmony with my femininity and appreciating all of what that meant. Now I had come full circle in this whole journey of the Eastern Parasite.

For the truly faithful, no miracle is necessary.
For those who doubt, no miracle is sufficient.

~ Nancy Gibbs

Owning the Knowing

Since the dream of the ruby bear-paw broach, I'd come a long way in my capacity to receive love. With this recent initiation back to the state of childlike acceptance I saw in several dreams that I was backtracking in order to clean up some of the damage done to my inner worlds when I'd imposed a magic spell on myself. This also meant that as I opened up to life and love, my relationship to the world was being redefined.

This dream brought to light a personality trait which was holding me back from receiving the fullness of Spirit's gifts.

I am living in a house with my ex-boyfriend. Two children are with us and it is well past their bedtime. I put them to bed and then begin to prepare a meal of leftover Chinese food.

A man enters the house. He is the owner and very attractive, regal and wealthy. He is embarrassed when he finds us in his home and for some reason offers us money. I see his clothes that are laid over a chair. They are exquisitely tailored and beautiful beyond anything I have ever seen, with gold chord on the shoulders

     Dream Yourself Awake

as if for a king. Realizing I am naked, I look for my clothes to get
dressed and leave but I have none. My ex-boyfriend has several
blue suitcases which I recognize to be my mother's, something she
gave him years ago.

In the dream, I am occupying a home that somehow seems familiar and of the past. My ex-boyfriend had been my first real love and the one relationship where I'd began to know the meaning of divine love. In many ways I had always held this relationship like a diamond of such high value that no other could come close.

The two children being kept up so late is the dream's way of telling me to put to rest my searching. The leftover Chinese food represents the Eastern Parasite's last foothold in my consciousness. It is time to bring to a completion the lesson of acceptance. Then the true owner returns – a representation of the higher side of my male nature. I have been introduced to him in other forms, in earlier dreams, as a promise of greater abundance and happiness in my life. The strange behaviour the man exhibits by giving us money when in fact we should be paying him, speaks of my own lesson of self-worth. I, like the nobleman, was oblivious to my own inner possessions. His richness reflects the attainment of spiritual wealth. The dream is saying that I haven't yet grasped who and what I am.

My nakedness and embarrassment in the dream express areas of my life where I have not taken possession of the qualities contained in the clothes which are lying dormant on the chair. The fine clothes were also seen in an earlier dream about the President but belonged to an elegant woman.

The blue suitcases were my mother's baggage which had been passed on to a male aspect of myself. They are of the mental realm which vibrates in blue tones.

A whole sequence of lesson concludes here including the one which began with the dream of the BMW some time before. In it, I was given the car and a key. To operate the vehicle I would have to find and master the state of consciousness the car represented. For the past several years I had been searching for the way to start this new vehicle through a mechanical formula.

I thought that if I said a few spiritually-charged words or did some extraordinary thing that I would find this formula. I discovered that the only formula was to claim my spiritual birthright. The way to the state of true ownership is through a relinquishing of doubt, shame and fear and through total trust in our relationship to Spirit.

Never forget that life can only be nobly inspired and
rightly lived if you take it bravely and gallantly,
as a splendid adventure in which you are setting out
into an unknown country, to face many a danger,
to meet many a joy, to find many a comrade,
to win and lose many a battle.

~ Annie Besant

The Stage of life

The interplay of lessons which had governed so many of my experiences over the last several years was finally winding down. I had often watched life from the edge of my seat prepared for the worst and many times playing the role of the victim.

Each of my dreams and experiences were slowly but surely mending an immense fracture in my relationship with the spiritual current, the parent and creative source of life.

It became evident that it was a pattern of not only belief, but feeling. I had felt a certain way for so long that I sought out the familiarity of that feeling. I had wanted to break free of the limitations which seemed to constrict my ability to have total good in my life. My inner guide used everyone and everything as my teacher in leading me back to trust.

Dreams were often rehearsals where I tried out a character, that I would later play in life. In this way I could see what lay ahead for me or how I could play that character differently. The way that dreams spread themselves out over time, like a movie script, fascinated me as I saw that life was a rehearsal for Soul to see the result of its choices in motion.

A friend told of an experience with her spouse. She had been making attempts to find more balance in her relationships. For a long time her emotions were intense and caused her a lot of grief.

One evening she found herself out of the body witnessing the creation of an emotion that she would then enter into.

Afterward she would be forced to experience the emotion without objectivity so that she could feel and experience the repercussions of that emotion. Back and forth she went between the two realities until she saw that Soul had created the entire experience. Nothing was outside herself. All creations were from Soul.

She also observed that each emotion spurred her partner to certain reflex reactions. For instance, if she needed him strongly, he automatically pulled away.

In this way the inner master gave her an experience which would eventfully help her in gaining self-mastery over her emotions.

Dreams are places where Soul can test drive a situation to determine if a lesson has really been learned.

The following dream shows how this works.

I am with a woman who is on her way somewhere. She wants me to follow her but I am not certain where she is going. I ask, "Will this journey take me closer to my real destination?" She avoids my question and once again tries to persuade me to go with her. Again I ask her if the journey will take me closer to my real destination. This time she avoids my question all together. Finally, I see that there is a great deal of snow and I say I cannot come for I have no shoes and have hurt my foot.

Dream Yourself Awake

The dream master was standing off to the side to watch how I would handle this test. One of the most prominent lessons of my life was that of losing direction through an outer influence. This does not make mastership material.

Each time we allow another to pull us off course we lose a little momentum, and our inner voice grows dimmer until we forget who we are and where we were going in the first place.

Other dreams are dress rehearsals for our outer life in that they prepare us in advance to detect the traps that might set us off balance. This way we can sidestep the creation of unnecessary karma if an outer situation does occur.

The following dream showed me how I was rehearsing for the real thing.

I'm on a flight destined for Europe, travelling with my mate. There is an emergency training session taking place right there on board as the passengers look on. A man is the trainer and he uses a flight attendant to show how someone might react in an emergency. She overacts though and is kicking so hard and close to me that I become annoyed and angry with her.

Afterwards my boyfriend and I are discussing our plans once we get to Europe. It seems he has friends and family he wishes to visit and I'm slightly ill at ease. I realize that everything will work out properly.

There were two separate yet interwoven themes that the dream master was demonstrating: The first had to do with trust in outcomes by listening to my inner, higher nature. The second shows how reacting to false problems was interfering in my development.

Europe represents the place overseas or across the great ocean of love to the true destination of Soul.

The future of our relationship as I moved forward towards my spiritual goals depended on my ability to surrender to Spirit in all my affairs. This quality of surrender determined my readiness to cross the borders into the true worlds of Soul.

I saw over the next while that my outer relationships were merely a reflection of my inner journey. By placing myself in the hands of an incompetent helmsman I could run aground or be taken far off course, eventually losing the taste for travel and adventure.

It is important to choose in whom we place our trust and most importantly to look for the qualities of Godliness in those we encounter on our journey.

Dream Yourself Awake

If you love, then all things will come to you. At some point love will begin to direct all your actions and thoughts. Then you can accept life.

~ Harold Klemp

The No-Power

It had been several months since my dream of being put in jail for doing magic on the Niagara River. Still some of the same lessons were recurring in my life. Money and trust were deeply linked. Scarcity and fear were close companions.

We must be economical even in how we speak about ourselves. I learned this the hard way.

One weekend I'd travelled to a seminar in Washington, D.C. I had counted on withdrawing funds from my bank account once I arrived as I'd expected some money to be deposited into my account on that date. In a conversation with a friend, I described myself in a negative tone by saying I didn't have a lot of money.

A few moments later when I found a bank machine and attempted to withdraw some money, I found that there was no money in my account. Immediately I saw the cause and effect relationship between my recent statement and this difficulty. In referring to myself as poor the universe had no choice but to give me exactly what I had asked.

Back at home a series of opportunities simply vanished

before my eyes leaving me astounded and dismayed at what I had interpreted as another roadblock to success.

That evening I spoke to a friend Janine telling her of my confusion. I simply couldn't comprehend why life refused to move forward.

That night I dreamt.

I'm at my friend Janine's place. I ask her what could be causing the problem. She hands me a deck of Tarot cards. I turn one over. On it is the word "Magic."

The dream stayed in the background of my consciousness throughout the rest of my sleep. I knew that in some way I had still failed to pass beyond the test of using magic. As I sat in contemplation I rolled over the idea of love and power.

I opened a book called, *In the Company of ECK Masters*, by Phil Morimitsu. The passage was a story about Zarathustra or Zoroaster. He describes the lesson of Soul in using manipulation and power.

"When the ego tries to direct the ECK (Spirit), no matter what the reason, it becomes manipulation and an indulgence in the black arts. The Masters talk of the no-power. We of ourselves have this tremendous power flowing through us, but we ourselves have no power. To claim It or try to grasp hold of It would be like trying to grasp electricity as it flows through the wires."

Relinquishing control was the seed of the lesson. I was to see that Spirit would have Its way, in Its own time and that it was a process of learning trust and true surrender. Because Spirit works for the good of everyone in the larger scope of life, It designs our experiences with the whole picture in mind.

Dream Yourself Awake

By hanging on so tightly to a concept of what Spirit had intended for my life's purpose I was limiting it to conditions.

Each job we are doing for Spirit is equal in the eyes of God. Learning to give without expectation while completely surrendering the idea of success or failure is part of the key. There are no failures in life, only lessons.

I had a grandiose vision of my importance in the universal scheme of life. Therefore I missed opportunities to give to life in the moment. This was one of the simple keys that Spirit was guiding me to understand – how the law of Gratitude, plays a role in the events of our life.

As I was put in a position of apparent success rather than some sort of illusion of failure, the charge connected to each slowly diminished.

A painful process, but in the end there was nothing that could be taken away from me that would cause me to lose my foothold in the higher worlds of God.

You can't compare yourself to anybody.
And you can't be in competition with yourself.
You just have to see what you love, open yourself up,
and do your best to put your hands on that jewel,
because it's going to radiate energy.

~ Barbara Sher

The Door to Freedom

Before I can bring closure to this book, it is necessary to disclose just how I finally came to have mastery over what was know as the Eastern Parasite.

From the first dream to the last the same theme emerged; that of learning to exert the creative power of Soul in all aspects of life. Each successive dream and life experience tore away the veils of the human consciousness which limited my ability to know and understand Soul's true destiny.

In the first dream of the waitress who wouldn't serve me, I was given the seed of the lesson: that of going beyond the limitations of chance, luck, and prediction to where Soul commands its own destiny here and now.

Waiting for fortune to arrive is a habit of lifetimes. We make our own fortune as the saying goes. The Eastern Parasite became more powerful each time I gave away my power to outside forces.

Only by finding the power to affirm and reaffirm my right as Soul to live, love and to be, no matter what the circumstances

Dream Yourself Awake

or authority, would I break the hold of this entity.

After a long search for some solid description of the Eastern Parasite, I understood that it was not an actual being but an energy. The energy was a warning whenever I let anyone or anything impose a restriction on Soul.

The main source of the Parasite's hold was through allowing others to command my life. Whether through unsolicited advice, undue criticism, envy, jealousy, anger or another, I had repeatedly opened myself to the energy which fed the Parasite.

In future dreams I was told how to find my source of strength and certainty through the one true unlimited Spirit. As long as I was united with this force, nothing could harm me.

The test of the Eastern Parasite was in learning not to give away power and energy. Several experiences explained how relying too much on positivity can trap Soul.

The dream of the owner of the house who feels he must pay to be there revealed one major area where energy was being lost. Our state of consciousness is our home. We need not diminish our expression to make others comfortable in our presence.

In opening to the greater expression of truth that was myself, accepting the magnificence of that expression and fully living in that, I found the door that led back to myself and freedom. Each dream was a letter to myself of that promise of freedom.

There is an eternal landscape, a geography of the soul; We search for its outline all our lives.

~ Josephine Hart

An Ever Present Love

When it comes to cycles, seasons or life-lessons, there are seldom precise moments when we can exactly define our arrival or exit from an experience. I often feel autumn's entrance somewhere in late July when the scent of brisk air currents begin to roll in. These minute changes which are occurring every moment of our lives slowly mold us into more graceful beings.

For a long time the goal of Self-Realization eluded me, until I learned that the key was in the ever-present awareness of absolute trust and certainty in Spirit's love and support.

My earlier dreams of Oprah created the impulse that spurred me on to find my own source of power as a woman and to live in simplicity and grace. Oprah is the maker of dreams. Wherever she gives her blessing other lives are improved.

We are all makers of each others' dreams. Some of us have the mission of assisting others to help shape their dreams and others the means to bring those dreams into reality.

As if to add an addendum to this book, Oprah appeared in a final dream. We discussed the stages I'd gone through in writing and rewriting this book over the last two years. I knew that what I had learned as a writer, dreamer and leader was coming to fruition. I turned to Oprah and said, "You know, I've really learned to love myself."

It is by committing ourselves to not only doing what we love but by "Being Love and serving life," as my friend Julie Olson so often says, that we finally cross the threshold of self-realization.

It may come as a quiet yet poignant moment where we simply know that we have completed that first leg of our journey towards God.

Life, as they say, holds no guarantees except that we can be certain of the ever-present love of Spirit in our lives. Living fully in our own awareness of this presence is its own reward.

About the Author

Darlene Montgomery is an internationally respected authority on dreams, spiritual perspectives and ideas. She is an author, speaker and clergywoman who speaks to groups and organizations on uplifting subjects. She is a recognized media personality having appeared in leading publications such as *Chicken Soup for the Parent's Soul*, CBC, NBC and others.

She is founder of Lifedreams Unlimited, a respected organization that produces inspirational seminars and books. Clients include fortune 500 companies, associations and organizations. To learn more about Darlene Montgomery's keynotes and seminars or for a personal coaching session visit <www.lifedreams.org> or call 416-696-1684.

Bibliography

Whitfield, Charles, *Healing the Child Within*, Health Communications 1987.

The Golden Dream, Heather Hughes-Calero, Coastline Publishing Company 1987.

The Flute of God, Paul Twitchell, ECKANKAR 1969.

Journey of Souls, Michael Newton, Ph. D., Llewellyn Publications 1994.

Notes From a Friend, Anthony Robins, Fireside Books 1995.

The Lessons of Love, Melody Beattie, Harper Collins 1994.

The Anatomy of Spirit, Caroline Myss, Crown Publishing 1996.

Anitya, Paul Twitchell, The Illuminated Way Press, 1969.

In the Company of ECK Masters, Phil Morimitsu, ECKANKAR, 1989.

Glossary

Chela.
(Chee-lah)

A spiritual student

Balance

Utilizing Edu-K's 5 steps to learning which regulate conflicts between structure and function.

Educational
Kinesiology
(Edu-K)

A process for drawing out innate learning abilities through the understanding of movement and its relationship to whole-brain patterns.

God-Realization

The state of God Consciousness. Complete and conscious awareness of God.

Hu
(Hyoo)

The most ancient, secret name for God. The singing of the word Hu is considered a love song to God. It can be sung aloud or silently to oneself.

Dream Yourself Awake

Planes.	*The levels of existence, such as Physical, Astral, Causal, Mental, Etheric or Soul Planes.*
Self-Realization, Soul Recognition	*The entering of Soul into the Soul Plane and there beholding Itself as pure Spirit. A state of seeing, knowing and being.*
Soul The True Self	*The inner, most sacred part of each person. Soul exists before birth and lives on after the death of the physical body. As a spark of God, Soul can see, know, and perceive all things. It is the creative center of Its own world.*
Spiritual Exercises	*The practice of spiritual techniques to open one to higher states of awareness and illumination.*

Darlene Montgomery